U.S. Department of Justice
Office of Justice Programs
National Institute of Justice

Guide for the Selection of Personal Protective Equipment for Emergency First Responders

NIJ Guide 102–00, Volume I

Dr. Alim A. Fatah[1]
John A. Barrett[2]
Richard D. Arcilesi, Jr.[2]
Charlotte H. Lattin[2]
Charles G. Janney[2]
Edward A. Blackman[2]

Coordination by:
Office of Law Enforcement Standards
National Institute of Standards and Technology
Gaithersburg, MD 20899–8102

Prepared for:
National Institute of Justice
Office of Science and Technology
Washington, DC 20531

November 2002

This document was prepared under CBIAC contract number SPO–900–94–D–0002 and Interagency Agreement M92361 between NIST and the Department of Defense Technical Information Center (DTIC).

NCJ 191518

---

[1]National Institute of Standards and Technology, Office of Law Enforcement Standards.

[2]Battelle Memorial Institute.

National Institute of Justice

Sarah V. Hart
Director

This guide was prepared for the National Institute of Justice, U.S. Department of Justice, by the Office of Law Enforcement Standards of the National Institute of Standards and Technology under Interagency Agreement 94–IJ–R–004, Project No. 99–060–CBW. It was also prepared under CBIAC contract No. SPO–900–94–D–0002 and Interagency Agreement M92361 between NIST and the Department of Defense Technical Information Center (DTIC).

The authors wish to thank Ms. Kathleen Higgins of the National Institute of Standards and Technology, Mr. Bill Haskell of SBCCOM, Ms. Priscilla S. Golden of General Physics, LTC Don Buley of the Joint Program Office of Biological Defense, Ms. Nicole Trudel of Camber Corporation, Dr. Stephen Morse of Centers for Disease Control, and Mr. Todd Brethauer of the Technical Support Working Group for their significant contributions to this effort. We would also like to acknowledge the Interagency Board for Equipment Standardization and Interoperability, which consists of Government and first responder representatives.

FOREWORD

NIJ is the research, development, and evaluation agency of the U.S. Department of Justice and is solely dedicated to researching crime control and justice issues. NIJ provides objective, independent, nonpartisan, evidence-based knowledge and tools to meet the challenges of crime and justice, particularly at the State and local levels.

The NIJ Director is appointed by the President and confirmed by the Senate. The Director establishes the Institute's objectives and is guided by the priorities of the Office of Justice Programs, the U.S. Department of Justice, and the needs of the field. The Institute actively solicits the views of criminal justice and other professionals and researchers to inform its search for the knowledge and tools to guide policy and practice.

In partnership with others, NIJ's mission is to prevent and reduce crime, improve law enforcement and the administration of justice, and promote public safety. By applying the disciplines of the social and physical sciences, NIJ:

- Researches the nature and impact of crime and delinquency.
- Develops applied technologies, standards, and tools for criminal justice practitioners.
- Evaluates existing programs and responses to crime.
- Tests innovative concepts and program models in the field.
- Assists policymakers, program partners, and justice agencies.
- Disseminates knowledge to many audiences.

As part of its standard development activities, NIJ serves as the executive agent for the Interagency Board for Equipment Standardization and Interoperability (IAB). The IAB has developed a set of priorities for standards for equipment to be used by first responders to critical incidents, including terrorist incidents relating to chemical, biological, nuclear, radiological, and explosive weapons. In particular, the development of chemical and biological defense equipment guides for the emergency first responder community is a high priority of NIJ.

The Office of Law Enforcement Standards (OLES) of the National Institute of Standards and Technology (NIST) furnishes technical support to NIJ in the development of standards. OLES subjects existing equipment to laboratory testing and evaluation and conducts research leading to the development of national standards, user guides, and technical reports.

This document covers research conducted by OLES under the sponsorship of NIJ. Other NIJ documents developed by OLES cover protective clothing and equipment, communications systems, emergency equipment, investigative aids, security systems, vehicles, weapons, analytical techniques, and standard reference materials used by the forensic community.

Technical comments and suggestions concerning this guide are invited from all interested parties. They may be addressed to the Office of Law Enforcement Standards, National Institute of Standards and Technology, 100 Bureau Drive, Stop 8102, Gaithersburg, MD 20899–8102.

Sarah V. Hart, Director
National Institute of Justice

iii

CONTENTS

TABLES

FIGURES

COMMONLY USED SYMBOLS AND ABBREVIATIONS

A	ampere	h	hour	oz	ounce
ac	alternating current	hf	high frequency	o.d.	outside diameter
AM	amplitude modulation	Hz	hertz	Ω	ohm
cd	candela	i.d.	inside diameter	p.	page
cm	centimeter	in	inch	Pa	pascal
CP	chemically pure	IR	infrared	pe	probable error
c/s	cycle per second	J	joule	pp.	pages
d	day	L	lambert	ppm	parts per million
dB	decibel	L	liter	qt	quart
dc	direct current	lb	pound	rad	radian
°C	degree Celsius	lbf	pound-force	rf	radio frequency
°F	degree Fahrenheit	lbf·in	pound-force inch	rh	relative humidity
dia	diameter	lm	lumen	s	second
emf	electromotive force	ln	logarithm (base e)	SD	standard deviation
eq	equation	log	logarithm (base 10)	sec.	Section
F	farad	M	molar	SWR	standing wave ratio
fc	footcandle	m	meter	uhf	ultrahigh frequency
fig.	Figure	μ	micron	UV	ultraviolet
FM	frequency modulation	min	minute	V	volt
ft	foot	mm	millimeter	vhf	very high frequency
ft/s	foot per second	mph	miles per hour	W	watt
g	acceleration	m/s	meter per second	N	newton
g	gram	mo	month	λ	wavelength
gal	gallon	N·m	newton meter	wk	week
gr	grain	nm	nanometer	wt	weight
H	henry	No.	number	yr	year

area=unit^2 (e.g., ft^2, in^2, etc.); volume=unit^3 (e.g., ft^3, m^3, etc.)

ACRONYMS SPECIFIC TO THIS DOCUMENT

ASTM	American Society for Testing and Materials	NIJ	National Institute of Justice
BW	Biological Warfare	NIOSH	National Institute for Occupational Safety and Health
CB	Chemical and Biological	NIST	National Institute of Standards and Technology
CBW	Chemical Biological Warfare	NATO	North Atlantic Treaty Organization
CPU	Collective Protective Undergarment	NBC	Nuclear, Biological, and Chemical
CW	Chemical Warfare	OSHA	Occupational Safety and Health Administration
DOD	Department of Defense	PAPR	Powered Air Purifying Respirator
DTAPS	Disposable Toxicological Agent Protective Suit	PF	Protection Factor
DPG	Dugway Proving Grounds	PICS	Personal Ice Cooling System
DRES	Defense Research Establishment Suffield	POL	Petroleum, Oils, and Lubricants
ECBE	Edgewood Chemical Biological Center, Aberdeen Proving Ground, MD	PPE	Personal Protective Equipment
EOD	Explosive Ordnance Disposal	PPV	Positive Pressure Ventilation
EPA	Environmental Protection Agency	PVC	Polyvinyl chloride
ERDEC	U.S. Army Edgewood Research, Development and Engineering Center	SBCCOM	U.S. Army Soldier and Biological Chemical Command
FBI	Federal Bureau of Investigation	SCBA	Self-Contained Breathing Apparatus
FR	Fire Resistant	SCFM	Standard Cubic Feet per Minute
HAZMAT	Hazardous Materials	STB	Super Tropical Bleach
IDLH	Immediately Dangerous to Life and Health	TAP	Toxicological Agent Protective
IAB	Interagency Board	TICs	Toxic Industrial Chemicals
ITAR	International Traffic and Arms Regulations	TIMs	Toxic Industrial Materials
NFPA	National Fire Protection Association	TOP	Test Operating Procedure

PREFIXES (See ASTM E380)

d	deci (10^{-1})	da	deka (10)
c	centi (10^{-2})	h	hecto (10^2)
m	milli (10^{-3})	k	kilo (10^3)
μ	micro (10^{-6})	M	mega (10^6)
n	nano (10^{-9})	G	giga (10^9)
p	pico (10^{-12})	T	tera (10^{12})

Temperature: $T_C = (T_F - 32) \times 5/9$

COMMON CONVERSIONS

0.30480 m =1ft	4.448222 N = lbf
25.4 mm = 1 in	1.355818 J =1 ft·lbf
0.4535924 kg = 1 lb	0.1129848 N m = lbf·in
0.06479891g = 1gr	14.59390 N/m =1 lbf/ft
0.9463529 L = 1 qt	6894.757 Pa = 1 lbf/in^2
3600000 J = 1 kW·hr	1.609344 km/h = mph

Temperature: $T_F = (T_C \times 9/5) + 32$

ABOUT THIS GUIDE

The National Institute of Justice is the focal point for providing support to State and local law enforcement agencies in the development of counterterrorism technology and standards, including technology needs for chemical and biological defense. In recognizing the needs of State and local emergency first responders, the Office of Law Enforcement Standards (OLES) at the National Institute of Standards and Technology (NIST), supported by the National Institute of Justice (NIJ), the Technical Support Working Group (TSWG), the U.S. Army Soldier and Biological Chemical Command, and the Interagency Board for Equipment Standardization and Interoperability (IAB), is developing chemical and biological defense equipment guides. The guides will focus on chemical and biological equipment in areas of detection, personal protection, decontamination, and communication. This document focuses specifically on assisting the emergency first responder community in the evaluation and purchase of personal protective equipment.

The long range plans include these goals: (1) subject existing personal protective equipment to laboratory testing and evaluation against a specified protocol, and (2) conduct research leading to the development of a series of documents, including national standards, user guides, and technical reports. It is anticipated that the testing, evaluation, and research processes will take several years to complete; therefore, the National Institute of Justice has developed this initial guide for the emergency first responder community in order to facilitate their evaluation and purchase of personal protective equipment.

In conjunction with this program, additional guides, as well as other documents, are being issued in the areas of chemical agent and toxic industrial material detection equipment, biological agent detection equipment, decontamination equipment, and communication equipment.

The information contained in this guide has been obtained through literature searches and market surveys. The vendors were contacted multiple times during the preparation of this guide to ensure data accuracy. In addition, the information is supplemented with test data obtained from other sources (e.g., Department of Defense), if available. It should also be noted that the purpose of this guide is not to provide recommendations but rather to serve as a means to provide information to the reader to compare and contrast commercially available personal protective equipment. *Reference herein to any specific commercial products, processes, or services by trade name, trademark, manufacturer, or otherwise does not necessarily constitute or imply its endorsement, recommendation, or favoring by the United States Government. The information and statements contained in this guide shall not be used for the purposes of advertising, nor to imply the endorsement or recommendation of the United States Government.*

With respect to information provided in this guide, neither the United States Government nor any of its employees make any warranty, expressed or implied, including but not limited to the warranties of merchantability and fitness for a particular purpose. Further, neither the United States Government nor any of its employees assume any legal liability or responsibility for the accuracy, completeness, or usefulness of any information, apparatus, product, or process disclosed.

Technical comments, suggestions, and product updates are encouraged from interested parties. They may be addressed to the Office of Law Enforcement Standards, National Institute of Standards and Technology, 100 Bureau Drive, Stop 8102, Gaithersburg, MD 20899–8102. It is anticipated that this guide will be updated periodically.

Questions relating to the specific personal protective items, respiratory and percutaneous (skin) protection, included in this document should be addressed directly to the proponent agencies or the equipment manufacturers. Contact information for each equipment item included in this guide can be found in Volume IIa (respiratory protection), Volume IIb (percutaneous protection––garments), and Volume IIc (percutaneous––other apparel).

GUIDE FOR THE SELECTION OF PERSONAL PROTECTIVE EQUIPMENT FOR EMERGENCY FIRST RESPONDERS

This guide includes information that is intended to assist the emergency first responder community in the evaluation and purchase of personal protective equipment (PPE). It includes a thorough market survey of personal protection technologies and commercially available equipment known to the authors as of April 2001. Brief technical discussions are presented that consider the principles of protection of several items. Readers finding this material too technical can omit this information while still making use of the rest of the guide, and readers desiring more technical detail can obtain it from the references listed in appendix B.

1. INTRODUCTION

The primary purpose of the *Guide for the Selection of Personal Protective Equipment for Emergency First Responders* is to provide emergency first responders with information to aid them in the selection of PPE, both respiratory protection and percutaneous (skin) protection. The guide is intended to be more practical than technical and provides information on a variety of factors that should be considered when purchasing and using PPE, including duration of protection, dexterity/mobility (how cumbersome is the equipment), launderability, and use/reuse, to name a few.

Due to the large number of PPE items identified, the guide is separated into four volumes. Volume I represents the actual guide, Volume IIa, Volume IIb, and Volume IIc serve as supplements to Volume I since they contain the PPE data sheets only. Volume IIa contains the data sheets for respiratory protection, Volume IIb contains the data sheets for protective garments, and Volume IIc contains the data sheets for other protective apparel (boots, gloves, hoods, and lab coats, etc.).

The remainder of this guide (Vol. I) is divided into several sections. Section 2 presents background information about the function of PPE, the components of personal protective ensembles, and the levels of protection. Section 3 provides an introduction to chemical agents, TIMs, and biological agents. Specifically, it discusses CB agents by providing overviews, physical and chemical properties, routes of entry, and symptoms. It also discusses the 98 TIMs that are considered in this guide. Section 4 presents an overview of respiratory protection equipment. Section 5 presents an overview of percutaneous protection equipment. Section 6 discusses the 12 characteristics and performance parameters that are used to evaluate PPE in this guide (referred to as selection factors in the remainder of this guide). These selection factors were compiled by a panel of experienced scientists and engineers with multiple years of experience with PPE, domestic preparedness, and identification of emergency first responder needs. The factors have also been shared with the emergency responder community in order to get their thoughts and comments. Section 7 presents comparative evaluation of available respiratory protection equipment. Section 8 presents comparative evaluation of available percutaneous protective equipment (garments). Section 9 presents a comparative evaluation of other available percutaneous protective equipment (apparel).

Three appendices are also included within this guide. Appendix A lists questions that could assist emergency first responders when selecting PPE. Appendix B lists the documents that were referenced in this guide. Appendix C provides the immediately dangerous to life and health (IDLH) values for the chemical agents and most of the TIMs that are listed.

2. PERSONAL PROTECTIVE EQUIPMENT

The intent of this section is to provide background information about the function of PPE, the components of personal protective ensembles, and the levels of protection provided by PPE.

2.1 The Purpose of Personal Protective Equipment (PPE)

The purpose of personal protective clothing and equipment is to shield or isolate individuals from the chemical, physical, and biological hazards that may be encountered during hazardous materials operations. During an emergency response, it is not always apparent when exposure occurs. Many toxic materials pose invisible hazards and offer no warning properties.

PPE must be worn whenever the wearer faces potential hazards arising from toxic exposure. Many activities associated with emergency operations that may require the wearing of PPE are presented below:

- **Site Survey:** Individuals conducting an initial investigation of a hazardous materials incident/accident site. These situations are usually characterized by a large degree of uncertainty and mandate the highest levels of protection.

- **Emergency Rescue:** Individuals entering a hazardous materials area for the purpose of removing an exposure victim. Special considerations must be given to how the selected protective clothing may affect the ability of the wearer to carry out rescue operations.

- **Hazard Mitigation:** Individuals entering a hazardous materials area to prevent a potential toxic release or to reduce the hazards from an existing release. Protective clothing must accommodate the required tasks without sacrificing adequate protection.

- **Monitoring/Supervision:** Individuals entering a hazardous materials area for the explicit purpose of observing and directing work operations or preventing unnecessary safety risks.

- **Decontamination:** Individuals providing decontamination support to personnel or equipment leaving the contaminated site.

It is important that responders realize that no single combination of protective equipment and clothing is capable of protecting against all hazards. Thus, PPE should always be used in conjunction with other protective methods. For example, proper decontamination and engineering or administrative controls should always be employed as additional measures for preventing exposure.

2.2 Components of Personal Protective Ensembles

The approach in selecting PPE must encompass an "ensemble" of clothing and equipment items, which are easily integrated to provide an appropriate level of protection while still allowing one to carry out activities involving hazardous materials. Components forming an effective protective

3

ensemble may incorporate a wide variety of protective equipment and clothing items. For the purpose of this guide, the evaluated items have been organized into the following three groups:

- Respiratory Equipment (e.g., air purifying respirators and supplied air respirators).
- Protective Garments (e.g., encapsulated suits, coveralls, and overgarments).
- Other Protective Apparel (e.g., protective hoods, boots, and gloves).

Two examples of items that are not specifically percutaneous apparel, but are included in this discussion, are tape and personal cooling systems. Figure 2–1 shows an example of ChemTape, from Kappler Safety Group. ChemTape is used to secure the wrist and ankle cuffs in all levels of protection except Level A. Figure 2–2 shows the Personal Ice Cooling System (PICS) from GEOMET Technologies, Inc. Although a PIC is not a percutaneous item, it does protect the user from heat stress when worn with protective garments.

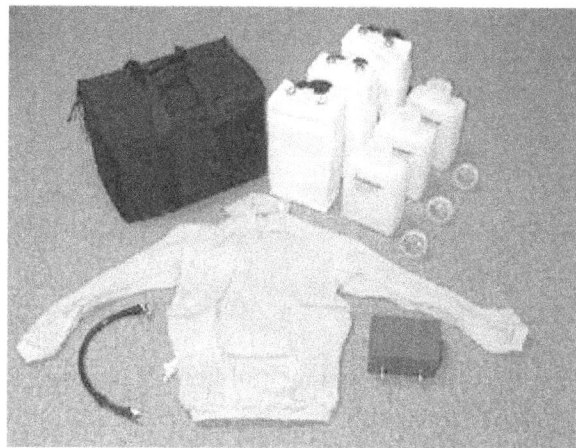

Figure 2–1. ChemTape, Kappler Safety Group

Figure 2–2. Personal Ice Cooling System (PICS) GEOMET Technologies, Inc.

The following figures are included to familiarize the reader with the types of protective apparel that are included in protective ensembles. Figure 2–3 is an example of a protective hood, the Tychem® TK hood/vest, pullover, PVC face shield, from DuPont Tyvek® Protective Apparel.

*Figure 2–3. Tychem® TK hood/vest, pullover, PVC
face shield, DuPont Tyvek® Protective Apparel*

Figure 2–4 and figure 2–5 are two examples of foot protection, the Bata boot/shoe covers from Bata Shoe Co., Inc. and the Tingley Hazproof Overboot from Tingley Rubber Corporation.

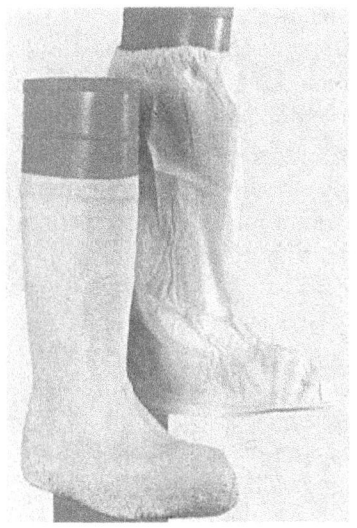

*2–4. Bata boot/shoe covers,
Bata Shoe Co., Inc.*

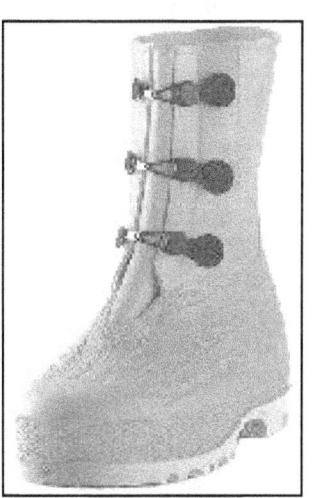

*Figure 2–5. Tingley Hazproof overboot,
Tingley Rubber Corporation*

Figure 2–6 and figure 2–7 offer two examples of hand and arm protection. They are the chemical protective butyl rubber gloves from Guardian Manufacturing Company, and the Lakeland Tychem® 9400 Level B Sleeves from Lakeland Industries, Inc.

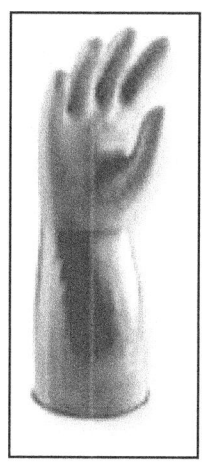

Figure 2–6. Chemical protective butyl rubber gloves, Guardian Manufacturing Co.

Figure 2–7. Lakeland Tychem® 9400 Level B Sleeves, Lakeland Industries, Inc.

2.3 Levels of Protection

It is important for responders to realize that selecting items based only on how they are designed or configured is not sufficient to ensure adequate protection. In other words, just having the right components to form an ensemble is not enough. The Environmental Protection Agency (EPA) levels of protection do not define what performance the selected clothing or equipment must offer. Many of these considerations are described in the "limiting criteria" column of table 2–1. Additional factors relevant to the various clothing and equipment items are described in subsequent sections.

Table 2–1 lists ensemble components based on the widely used EPA Levels of Protection (i.e., Levels A, B, C, and D). These lists can be used as the starting point for ensemble creation; however, each ensemble must be tailored to the specific situation in order to provide the most appropriate level of protection.

In addition to the EPA Levels of Protection, the National Fire Protection Agency (NFPA) has classified suits by their performance.

NFPA Standard 1991—Vapor-protective suits that provide "gas-tight" integrity and are intended for response situations where no chemical contact is permissible. This type of suit would be equivalent to EPA Level A protection.

NFPA Standard 1992—Liquid splash-protective suits offer protection against liquid chemicals in the form of splashes, but not against continuous liquid contact or chemical vapors or gases. This type of clothing would meet the EPA Level B needs.

NFPA Standard 1993—Support function protective garments that provide liquid splash protection but offer limited physical protection. They are intended for use in non-emergency, nonflammable situations where the chemical hazards have been completely characterized. Support function protective garments should not be used in chemical emergency response or in situations where chemical hazards remain uncharacterized.

Table 2–1. EPA levels of protection for ensemble components

Level A	Vapor protective suit (meets NFPA 1991) Pressure-demand, full-face SCBA, inner chemical-resistant gloves, and chemical-resistant safety boots.
	OPTIONAL: Cooling system, outer gloves, hard hat, and two-way radio communications system.
	Protection Provided: Highest available level of respiratory, skin, and eye protection from solid, liquid, and gaseous chemicals.
	Used When: The chemical(s) have been identified and pose high levels of hazards to respiratory system, skin, and eyes. Substances are present with known or suspected skin toxicity or carcinogenity. Operations must be conducted in confined or poorly ventilated areas.
	Limitations: Protective clothing must resist permeation by the chemical or mixtures present. Ensemble items must allow integration without loss of performance.
Level B	Liquid splash protective suit (meets NFPA 1992). Pressure demand, full facepiece SCBA, inner chemical-resistant gloves, chemical-resistant safety boots, and hard hat.
	OPTIONAL: Cooling system, outer gloves, and two-way radio communications system.
	Protection Provided: Provides same level of respiratory protection as Level A, but less skin protection. Liquid splash protection, but no protection against chemical vapors or gases.
	Used When: The chemical(s) have been identified but do not require a high level of skin protection. Initial site surveys are required until higher levels of hazards are identified. The primary hazards associated with site entry are from liquid and not vapor contact.
	Limitations: Protective clothing items must resist penetration by the chemicals or mixtures present. Ensemble items must allow integration without loss of performance.
Level C	***Not Acceptable for Chemical Emergency Response***
	Support Function Protective Garment (meets NFPA 1993). Full facepiece, air purifying, canister-equipped respirator, chemical-resistant gloves and safety boots, two-way radio communications system, and hard hat.
	OPTIONAL: Face shield, and escape SCBA.
	Protection Provided: Provides the same level of skin protection as Level B, but a lower level of respiratory protection. Liquid splash protection, but no protection against chemical vapors or gases.
	Used When: Contact with site chemical(s) will not affect the skin. Air contaminants have been identified and concentrations measured. A respirator canister is available that can remove the contaminant. The site and its hazards have been completely characterized.
	Limitations: Protective clothing items must resist penetration by the chemical or mixtures present. Chemical airborne concentration must be less than IDLH levels. The atmosphere must contain at least 19.5 % oxygen.
Level D	***Not Acceptable for Chemical Emergency Response***
	Coveralls, safety boots/shoes, safety glasses or chemical splash goggles.
	OPTIONAL: Gloves, escape SCBA, and face shield.
	Protection Provided: No respiratory protection, and minimal skin protection.
	Used When: The atmosphere contains no known hazards. Work functions preclude splashes, immersion, potential for inhalation, or direct contact with hazard chemicals.
	Limitations: This level should not be worn in the Hot Zone. The atmosphere must contain at least 19.5 % oxygen.

3. INTRODUCTION TO CHEMICAL WARFARE AGENTS, TOXIC INDUSTRIAL MATERIALS, AND BIOLOGICAL AGENTS

The purpose of this section is to provide a description of chemical warfare agents (CWA), toxic industrial materials (TIMs), and biological agents (BA).

3.1 Chemical Warfare Agents

Chemical warfare agents are chemical substances that are intended for use in warfare or terrorist activities to kill, seriously injure, or seriously incapacitate people through their physiological effects. A chemical agent attacks the organs of the human body, preventing the organs from functioning normally. The results are usually disabling or fatal. The volatility of a chemical agent often determines how it is used. Volatility refers to a substance's ability to become a vapor at a relatively low temperature. A highly volatile (nonpersistent) substance poses a greater respiratory hazard than a less volatile (persistent) substance.

The most common chemical warfare agents are the **nerve agents**, GA (Tabun), GB (Sarin), GD (Soman), GF, and VX; and the **blister agents**, HD (sulfur mustard) and HN (nitrogen mustard) and the arsenical vesicants, L (Lewisite). Other toxic chemicals such as hydrogen cyanide (characterized as a chemical **blood agent** by the military) are included as TIMs under section 3.2 of this guide. There are also toxic chemicals derived from living organisms, generically termed **toxins**. Toxins are included under section 3.3 of this guide.

3.1.1 Nerve Agents

This section provides an overview of nerve agents. A discussion of their physical and chemical properties, their routes of entry, and descriptions of symptoms is also provided.

3.1.1.1 Overview

Among lethal chemical agents, nerve agents have had an entirely dominant role since World War II. Nerve agents acquired their name because they affect the transmission of impulses in the nervous system. All nerve agents belong to the chemical group of organo-phosphorus compounds; many common herbicides and pesticides also belong to this chemical group. Nerve agents are stable, easily dispersed, highly toxic, and have rapid effects when absorbed both through the skin and the respiratory system. Nerve agents can be manufactured by means of fairly simple chemical techniques. The raw materials are inexpensive but some are subject to the controls of the Chemical Weapons Convention and the Australia Group Agreement.

3.1.1.2 Physical and Chemical Properties

The nerve agents considered in this guide are:

- GA: A low volatility persistent chemical agent that is taken up through skin contact and inhalation of the substance as a gas or aerosol.
- GB: A volatile nonpersistent chemical agent mainly taken up through inhalation.

- GD: A moderately volatile chemical agent that can be taken up by inhalation or skin contact.
- GF: A low volatility persistent chemical agent that is taken up through skin contact and inhalation of the substance either as a gas or aerosol.
- VX: A low volatility persistent chemical agent that can remain on material, equipment, and terrain for long periods. Uptake is mainly through the skin but also through inhalation of the substance as a gas or aerosol.

Nerve agents in the pure state are colorless liquids. Their volatility varies widely. The consistency of VX may be likened to motor oil and is therefore classified as belonging to the group of persistent chemical agents. Its effect is mainly through direct contact with the skin. GB is at the opposite extreme; being an easily volatile liquid (comparable with, e.g., water), it is mainly taken up through the respiratory organs. The volatilities of GD, GA, and GF are between those of GB and VX. Table 3–1 lists the common nerve agents and some of their physical and chemical properties. Water is included in the table as a reference point for the nerve agents.

Table 3–1. Physical and chemical properties of common nerve agents

Property	GA	GB	GD	GF	VX	Water
Molecular Weight	162.3	140.1	182.2	180.2	267.4	18
Density, g/cm^3 *	1.073	1.089	1.022	1.120	1.008	1
Boiling-point, °F	464	316	388	462	568	212
Melting-point, °F	18	-69	-44	-22	< -60	32
Vapor pressure, Mm Hg *	0.07	2.9	0.4	0.06	0.0007	23.756
Volatility, mg/m^3 *	610	22000	3900	600	10.5	23010
Solubility in Water, % *	10	Miscible with water	2	~2	Slightly	NA

*at 77 °F

3.1.1.3 Route of Entry

Nerve agents, either as a gas, aerosol, or liquid, enter the body through inhalation or through the skin. Poisoning may also occur through consumption of liquids or foods contaminated with nerve agents.

The route of entry also influences the symptoms developed and, to some extent, the sequence of the different symptoms. Generally, the poisoning works most rapidly when the agent is absorbed through the respiratory system rather than other routes because the lungs contain numerous blood vessels and the inhaled nerve agent can quickly diffuse into the blood circulation and thus reach the target organs. Among these organs, the respiratory system is one of the most important. If a person is exposed to a high concentration of nerve agent, e.g., 200 mg sarin/m^3, death may occur within a couple of minutes.

The poisoning works slower when the agent is absorbed through the skin. Since nerve agents are somewhat fat-soluble, they can easily penetrate the outer layers of the skin, but it takes longer for the poison to reach the deeper blood vessels. Consequently, the first symptoms do not occur until 20 min to 30 min after the initial exposure but subsequently, the poisoning process may be rapid if the total dose of nerve agent is high.

3.1.1.4 Symptoms

When exposed to a low dose of nerve agent, sufficient to cause minor poisoning, the victim experiences characteristic symptoms such as increased production of saliva, a runny nose, and a feeling of pressure on the chest. The pupil of the eye becomes contracted (miosis), which impairs night-vision. In addition, the capacity of the eye to change focal length is reduced, and short-range vision deteriorates causing the victim to feel pain when trying to focus on nearby objects. This is accompanied by a headache. Less specific symptoms are tiredness, slurred speech, hallucinations, and nausea.

Exposure to a higher dose leads to more dramatic developments, and symptoms are more pronounced. Bronchoconstriction and secretion of mucus in the respiratory system leads to difficulty in breathing and to coughing. Discomfort in the gastrointestinal tract may develop into cramping and vomiting, and there may be involuntary discharge of urine and feces. There may be excessive salivating, tearing, and sweating. If the poisoning is moderate, typical symptoms affecting the skeletal muscles may be muscular weakness, local tremors, or convulsions.

When exposed to a high dose of nerve agent, the muscular symptoms are more pronounced and the victim may suffer convulsions and lose consciousness. The poisoning process may be so rapid that symptoms mentioned earlier may never have time to develop.

Nerve agents affect the respiratory muscles causing muscular paralysis. Nerve agents also affect the respiratory center of the central nervous system. The combination of these two effects is the direct cause of death. Consequently, death caused by nerve agents is similar to death by suffocation.

3.1.2 Blister Agents (Vesicants)

This section provides an overview of blister agents. A discussion of their physical and chemical properties, their routes of entry, and descriptions of symptoms is also provided.

3.1.2.1 Overview

There are two major families of blister agents (vesicants): sulfur mustard (HD) and nitrogen mustard (HN), and the arsenical vesicants (L). All blister agents are persistent and may be employed in the form of colorless gases and liquids. They burn and blister the skin or any other part of the body they contact. Blister agents are likely to be used to produce casualties rather than to kill, although exposure to such agents can be fatal.

3.1.2.2 Physical and Chemical Properties

In its pure state, mustard agent is colorless and almost odorless. It earned its name as a result of an early production method that resulted in an impure product with a mustard-like odor. Mustard agent is also claimed to have a characteristic odor similar to rotten onions. However, the sense of smell is dulled after only a few breaths so that the smell can no longer be distinguished. In addition, mustard agent can cause injury to the respiratory system in concentrations that are so low that the human sense of smell cannot distinguish them.

At room temperature, mustard agent is a liquid with low volatility and is very stable during storage. Mustard agent can easily be dissolved in most organic solvents but has negligible solubility in water. In aqueous solutions, mustard agent decomposes into nonpoisonous products by means of hydrolysis but since only dissolved mustard agent reacts, the decomposition proceeds very slowly. Oxidants such as chloramines, however, react violently with mustard agent, forming nonpoisonous oxidation products. Consequently, these substances are used for the decontamination of mustard agent.

Arsenical vesicants are not as common or as stable as the sulfur or nitrogen mustards. All arsenical vesicants are colorless to brown liquids. They are more volatile than mustard and have fruity to geranium-like odors. These types of vesicants are much more dangerous as liquids than as vapors. Absorption of either vapor or liquid through the skin in adequate dosage may lead to systemic intoxication or death. The physical and chemical properties of the most common blister agents are listed in table 3–2. Water is included in the table as a reference point for the blister agents.

Table 3–2. Physical and chemical properties of common blister agents

Property	HD	HN-1	HN-2	HN-3	L	Water
Molecular Weight	159.1	170.1	156.1	204.5	207.4	18
Density, g/cm^3	1.27 at 68 °F	1.09 at 77 °F	1.15 at 68 °F	1.24 at 77 °F	1.89 at 68 °F	1 at 77 °F
Boiling-point, °F	421	381	167 at 15 mm Hg	493	374	212
Freezing-point, °F	58	-61.2	-85	-26.7	64.4 to 32.18	32
Vapor pressure, Mm Hg	0.072 at 68 °F	0.24 at 77 °F	0.29 at 68 °F	0.0109 at 77 °F	0.394 at 68 °F	23.756 at 77 °F
Volatility, mg/m^3	610 at 68 °F	1520 at 68 °F	3580 at 77 °F	121 at 77 °F	4480 at 68 °F	23010 at 77 °F
Solubility in Water, %	<1 %	Sparingly	Sparingly	Insoluble	Insoluble	NA

3.1.2.3 Route of Entry

Most blister agents are relatively persistent and are readily absorbed by all parts of the body. Poisoning may also occur through consumption of liquids or foods contaminated with blister agents. These agents cause inflammation, blisters, and general destruction of tissues. In the form of gas or liquid, mustard agent attacks the skin, eyes, lungs, and gastrointestinal tract. Internal organs, mainly blood-generating organs (i.e., bone marrow, spleen, and lymphatic tissue), may also be injured as a result of mustard agents being taken up through the skin or lungs and transported into the body. Since mustard agents give no immediate symptoms upon contact, a delay of between 2 h and 24 h may occur before pain is felt and the victim becomes aware of what has happened. By then, cell damage has already occurred. The delayed effect is a characteristic of mustard agent.

3.1.2.4 Symptoms

In general, vesicants can penetrate the skin by contact with either liquid or vapor. The latent period for the effects from mustard is usually several hours (the onset of symptoms from vapors is 4 h to 6 h and the onset of symptoms from skin exposure is 2 h to 48 h). There is no latent period for exposure to Lewisite.

Mild symptoms of mustard agent poisoning may include aching eyes with excessive tearing, inflammation of the skin, irritation of the mucous membranes, hoarseness, coughing, and sneezing. Normally, these injuries do not require medical treatment.

Severe injuries that are incapacitating and require medical care may involve eye injuries with loss of sight, the formation of blisters on the skin, nausea, vomiting, and diarrhea together with severe difficulty in breathing. Severe damage to the eye may lead to the total loss of vision.

The most pronounced effects on inner organs are injury to the bone marrow, spleen, and lymphatic tissue. This may cause a drastic reduction in the number of white blood cells 5 d to 10 d after exposure; a condition very similar to that after exposure to radiation. This reduction of the immune defense will complicate the already large risk of infection in people with severe skin and lung injuries.

The most common cause of death as a result of mustard agent poisoning is complications after lung injury caused by inhalation of mustard agent. Most of the chronic and late effects from mustard agent poisoning are also caused by lung injuries.

3.2 Toxic Industrial Materials (TIMs)

This section provides a general overview of TIMs as well as a list of the specific TIMs considered in this guide. Since the chemistry of TIMs is so varied, it is not feasible to discuss specific routes of entry and descriptions of symptoms. Several documents, including *2000 Emergency Response Guidebook (A Guidebook for First Responders During the Initial Phase of a Dangerous Goods/Hazardous Materials Incident)*, provide more detailed information about TIMs (see app. B).

TIMs are chemicals other than chemical warfare agents that have harmful effects on humans. TIMs, often referred to as toxic industrial chemicals, or TICs, are used in a variety of settings such as manufacturing facilities, maintenance areas, and general storage areas. While exposure to some of these chemicals may not be immediately dangerous to life and health (IDLH), these compounds may have extremely serious effects on an individual's health after multiple low-level exposures.

3.2.1 General

A TIM is a *specific type* of industrial chemical, i.e., one that has a LCt_{50} value (lethal concentration of a chemical vapor or aerosol for 50 % of the population multiplied by exposure time) less than 100000 mg-min/m^3 in any mammalian species and is produced in quantities exceeding 30 tons per year at one production facility. Although they are not as lethal as the highly toxic nerve agents, their ability to make a significant impact on the populace is assumed to be more related to the amount of chemical a terrorist can employ on the target(s) and less related to their lethality. None of these compounds are as highly toxic as the nerve agents, but they are produced in very large quantities (multi-ton) and are readily available; therefore, they pose a far greater threat than chemical warfare agents. For instance, sulfuric acid is not as lethal as the nerve agents, but it is easier to disseminate large quantities of sulfuric acid because large amounts of it are manufactured and transported everyday. It is assumed that a balance is struck between the lethality of a material and the amount of materials produced worldwide. Materials such as the nerve agents are so lethal as to be in a special class of chemicals.

Since TIMs are less lethal than the highly toxic nerve agents, it is more difficult to determine how to rank their potential for use by a terrorist. Physical and chemical properties for TIMs such as ammonia, chlorine, cyanogen chloride, and hydrogen cyanide are presented in table 3–3. Water is included in the table as a reference point for the TIMs. The physical and chemical properties for the remaining TIMs identified in this guide can be found in International *Task Force 25: Hazard From Industrial Chemicals Final Report, April 1998* (see app. B).

Table 3–3. Physical and chemical properties of TIMs

Property	Ammonia	Chlorine	Cyanogen Chloride	Hydrogen Cyanide	Water
Molecular weight	17.03	70.9	61.48	27.02	18
Density, g/cm^3	0.00077 at 77 °F	3.214 at 77 °F	1.18 at 68 °F	0.990 at 68 °F	1 at 77 °F
Boiling-point, °F	-28	-30	55	78	212
Freezing-point, °F	-108	-150	20	8	32
Vapor pressure, Mm Hg at 77 °F	7408	5643	1000	742	23.756
Volatility, mg/m^3	6782064 at 77 °F	21508124 at 77 °F	2600000 at 68 °F	1080000 at 77 °F	23010 at 77 °F
Solubility in water, %	89.9	1.5	Slightly	Highly soluble	NA

3.2.2 TIM Rankings

TIMs are ranked into one of three categories that indicate their relative importance and assist in hazard assessment. Table 3–4 lists the TIMs with respect to their hazard index ranking (high, medium, or low hazard).[3]

---

[3] Summary of the Final Report of the International Task Force 25 Hazard from Industrial Chemicals, 15 April 1999.

3.2.2.1 High Hazard

High hazard indicates a widely produced, stored or transported TIM, that has high toxicity and is easily vaporized.

3.2.2.2 Medium Hazard

Medium hazard indicates a TIM, which may rank high in some categories but lower in others such as number of producers, physical state, or toxicity.

3.2.2.3 Low Hazard

A low hazard overall ranking indicates that this TIM is not likely to be a hazard unless specific operational factors indicate otherwise.

Table 3–4. TIMs listed by hazard index

High	Medium	Low
Ammonia	Acetone cyanohydrin	Allyl isothiocyanate
Arsine	Acrolein	Arsenic trichloride
Boron trichloride	Acrylonitrile	Bromine
Boron trifluoride	Allyl alcohol	Bromine chloride
Carbon disulfide	Allylamine	Bromine pentafluoride
Chlorine	Allyl chlorocarbonate	Bromine trifluoride
Diborane	Boron tribromide	Carbonyl fluoride
Ethylene oxide	Carbon monoxide	Chlorine pentafluoride
Fluorine	Carbonyl sulfide	Chlorine trifluoride
Formaldehyde	Chloroacetone	Chloroacetaldehyde
Hydrogen bromide	Chloroacetonitrile	Chloroacetyl chloride
Hydrogen chloride	Chlorosulfonic acid	Crotonaldehyde
Hydrogen cyanide	Diketene	Cyanogen chloride
Hydrogen fluoride	1,2-Dimethylhydrazine	Dimethyl sulfate
Hydrogen sulfide	Ethylene dibromide	Diphenylmethane-4,4'-diisocyanate
Nitric acid, fuming	Hydrogen selenide	Ethyl chloroformate
Phosgene	Methanesulfonyl chloride	Ethyl chlorothioformate
Phosphorus trichloride	Methyl bromide	Ethyl phosphonothioic dichloride
Sulfur dioxide	Methyl chloroformate	Ethyl phosphonic dichloride
Sulfuric acid	Methyl chlorosilane	Ethyleneimine
Tungsten hexafluoride	Methyl hydrazine	Hexachlorocyclopentadiene
	Methyl isocyanate	Hydrogen iodide
	Methyl mercaptan	Iron pentacarbonyl
	Nitrogen dioxide	Isobutyl chloroformate
	Phosphine	Isopropyl chloroformate
	Phosphorus oxychloride	Isopropyl isocyanate
	Phosphorus pentafluoride	n-Butyl chloroformate
	Selenium hexafluoride	n-Butyl isocyanate
	Silicon tetrafluoride	Nitric oxide
	Stibine	n-Propyl chloroformate
	Sulfur trioxide	Parathion
	Sulfuryl chloride	Perchloromethyl mercaptan
	Sulfuryl fluoride	sec-Butyl chloroformate
	Tellurium hexafluoride	tert-Butyl isocyanate
	n-Octyl mercaptan	Tetraethyl lead
	Titanium tetrachloride	Tetraethyl pyroposphate
	Trichloroacetyl chloride	Tetramethyl lead
	Trifluoroacetyl chloride	Toluene 2,4-diisocyanate
		Toluene 2,6-diisocyanate

16

3.3 Biological Agents

The purpose of this section is to provide a description of the biological agents likely to be used in a terrorist attack. There are four categories under discussion: bacterial agents, viral agents, rickettsiae, and biological toxins.

3.3.1 Bacterial Agents

Bacteria are small, single-celled organisms, most of which can be grown on solid or liquid culture media. Under special circumstances, some types of bacteria can transform into spores that are more resistant to cold, heat, drying, chemicals, and radiation than the bacterium itself. Most bacteria do not cause disease in human beings but those that do cause disease by two differing mechanisms: by invading the tissues or by producing poisons (toxins). Many bacteria, such as anthrax, have properties that make them attractive as potential warfare agents:

- Retained potency during growth and processing to the end product (biological weapon).
- Long "shelf-life."
- Low biological decay as an aerosol.

Other bacteria require stabilizers to improve their potential for use as biological weapons. Table 3–5 lists some of the common bacterial agents along with possible methods of dissemination, incubation period, symptoms, and treatment.

3.3.2 Viral Agents

Viruses are the simplest type of microorganism and consist of a nucleocapsid protein coat containing genetic material, either RNA or DNA. Because viruses lack a system for their own metabolism, they require living hosts (cells of an infected organism) for replication. As biological agents, they are attractive because many do not respond to antibiotics. However, their incubation periods are normally longer than for other biological agents, so incapacitation of victims may be delayed. Table 3–6 lists the common viral agents along with possible methods of dissemination, incubation period, symptoms, and treatment.

3.3.3 Rickettsiae

Rickettsiae are obligate intracellular bacteria that are intermediate in size between most bacteria and viruses and possess certain characteristics common to both bacteria and viruses. Like bacteria, they have metabolic enzymes and cell membranes, use oxygen, and are susceptible to broad-spectrum antibiotics, but like viruses, they grow only in living cells. Most rickettsiae can be spread only through the bite of infected insects and are not spread through human contact. Table 3–7 lists the common rickettsiae along with possible methods of dissemination, incubation periods, symptoms, and treatment.

3.3.4 Biological Toxins

Biological toxins are poisons produced by living organisms. It is the poison and not the organism that produces harmful effects in man. A toxin typically develops naturally in a host organism (for example, saxitoxin is produced by marine algae); however, genetically altered and/or synthetically manufactured toxins have been produced in a laboratory environment. Biological toxins are most similar to chemical agents in their dissemination and effectiveness. Table 3–8 lists the common biological toxins along with possible methods of dissemination, incubation period, symptoms, and treatment.

Table 3–5. Bacterial agents

Biological Agent/Disease	Anthrax	Brucellosis	E. coli serotype (O157:H7)	Tularemia	Cholera
Likely Method of Dissemination	1. Spores in aerosol 2. Sabotage (food)	1. Aerosol 2. Sabotage (food)	Water and food supply contamination	1. Aerosol 2. Rabbits or ticks	1. Sabotage (food and water) 2. Aerosol
Transmissible Person to Person	No (except cutaneous)	Unknown	Unknown, evidence passed person-to-person in day-care or nursing homes	No	Rare
Incubation Period	1 d to 43 d	1 wk to 3 wk, sometimes months	Unknown	2 d to 10 d	3 d to 5 d
Duration of Illness	3 d to 5 d (usually fatal)	Unknown	5 d to 10 d (most cases)	>2 wk	>1 wk
Lethality	Contact or cutaneous anthrax: fatality rate of 5 % to 20 % Inhalational anthrax: after symptoms appear almost always fatal, regardless of treatment	Low	Fatality rate is 0 % to 15 % if victim develops hemolytic uremic syndrome (HUS); 5 % if victim develops thrombotic thrombocytopenic purpura (TTP)	Moderate if left untreated	Low (<1 %) with treatment; high (>50 %) without
Vaccine Efficacy (for aerosol exposure)/ Antitoxin	Currently no human data	Vaccine under evaluation	No vaccine	No commercially available vaccine	No data on aerosol
Symptoms and Effects	Flu-like, upper-respiratory distress; fever and shock in 3 d to 5 d, followed by death	Irregular prolonged fever, profuse sweating, chills, joint and muscle pain, persistent fatigue	Gastrointestinal (diarrhea, vomiting) dehydration; in severe cases, cardiac arrest and death, HUS, or TTP	Chills, sustained fever, prostration, tendency for pneumonia, enlarged, painful lymph nodes, headache, malaise, anorexia, non-productive cough	Sudden onset with nausea, vomiting, diarrhea, rapid dehydration, toxemia and collapse
Treatment	Vaccine available for cutaneous, possibly inhalation, anthrax. Cutaneous anthrax responds to antibiotics (penicillin, terramycin, chloromycetin), sulfa-diazine and immune serum. Pulmonary (inhaled) anthrax responds to immune serum in initial stages but is little use after disease is well established. Intestinal, same as for pulmonary	Antibiotics	Antibiotics available; most recover without antibiotics within 5 d to 10 d; do not use antidiarrheal agents	Vaccination using live attenuated organisms reduces severity and transmittability; antibiotics (streptomycin, aureomycin, chloromycetin, doxycycline, tetracycline, and chloramphenical)	Replenish fluids and electrolytes; antibiotics (tetracycline, ciprofloxicin, and erythromycin) enhance effectiveness of rehydration and reduce organism in body
Potential as Biological Agent	High, Iraqi and USSR biological programs worked to develop anthrax as a bio-weapon	Unknown	Unknown	High, if delivered via aerosol form (highly infectious, 90 % to 100 %)	Not appropriate for aerosol delivery

Table 3–5. Bacterial agents–Continued

Biological Agent/Disease	Diphtheria	Glanders	Melioidosis	Plague (Bubonic and Pneumonic)	Typhoid Fever
Likely Method of Dissemination	Unknown	1. Aerosol 2. Cutaneous	1. Food contamination (rodent feces) 2. Inhalation 3. Insect bites 4. Direct contact with infected animals	1. Infected fleas (Bubonic and Pneumonic) 2. Aerosol (Pneumonic)	1. Contact with infected person 2. Contact with contaminated substances
Transmissible Person to Person	High	High	No	High (Pneumonic)	High
Incubation Period	2 d to 5 d	3 d to 5 d	Days	1 d to 3 d	7 d to 14 d
Duration of Illness	Unknown	Unknown	4 d to 20 d	1 d to 6 d (usually fatal)	Unknown
Lethality	5 % to 10 % fatality	50 % to 70 %	Variable	5 % to 10 % if treated; Bubonic: 30 % to 75 % if untreated Pneumonic: 95 % if untreated	<1 % if treated 10 % to 14 % if untreated
Vaccine Efficacy (for aerosol exposure)/ Antitoxin	DPT vaccine 85 % effective; booster recommended every 10 yr	No vaccine	No vaccine	Vaccine not available	Oral vaccine (Vivotif) and single dose injectable vaccine (capsular poly-saccharide antigen); both vaccines are equally effective and offer 65 % to 75 % protection against the disease
Symptoms and Effects	Local infection usually in respiratory passages; delay in treatment can cause damage to heart, kidneys, and central nervous system	Skin lesions, ulcers in skin, mucous membranes, and viscera; if inhaled, upper respiratory tract involvement	Cough, fever, chills, muscle/joint pain, nausea, and vomiting; progressing to death	Enlarged lymph nodes in groin; septicemic (spleen, lungs, meninges affected)	Prolonged fever, lymph tissue involvement; ulceration of intestines; enlargement of spleen; rose-colored spots on skin; constipation or diarrhea
Treatment	Antitoxin extremely effective; antibiotic (penicillin) shortens the duration of illness	Drug therapy (streptomycin and sulfadiazine) is somewhat effective	Antibiotics (doxycycline, chlorothenicol, tetracycline), and sulfadiazine	Doxycycline (100 mg 2x/d for 7 d); ciprofloxicin also effective	Antibiotics (amoxicillin or cotrimoxazole) shorten period of communicability and cure disease rapidly
Potential as Biological Agent	Very low—symptoms not severe enough to incapacitate; rare cases of severe infection	Unknown	Moderate—rare disease, no vaccine available	High—highly infectious, particularly in pneumonic (aerosol) form; lack of stability and loss of virulence complicate its use	Not likely to be deployed via aerosol; more likely for covert contamination of water or food.

Table 3–6. Viral agents

Biological Agent/Disease	Marburg Virus	Junin Virus	Rift Valley Fever Virus	Smallpox	Venezuelan Equine Encephalitis
Likely Method of Dissemination	Aerosol	Epidemiology not known	Mosquito-borne; in biological scenario, aerosols or droplets	Aerosol	1. Aerosol 2. Infected vectors
Transmissible Person to Person	Unknown	Unknown	Unknown	High	No
Incubation Period	5 d to 7 d	7 d to 16 d	2 d to 5 d	10 d to 12 d	1 d to 6 d
Duration of Illness	Unknown	16 d	2 d to 5 d	4 wk	Days to weeks
Lethality	25 %	18 %	<1 %	20 % to 40 % (Viriole major) <1 % (Viriole minor)	1 % to 60 %
Vaccine Efficacy (for aerosol exposure)/ Antitoxin	No vaccine	No vaccine	Inactivated vaccine available in limited quantities	Vaccine protects against infection within 3 d to 5 d of exposure	Experimental only: TC–83 protects against 30 LD_{50}s to 500 LD_{50}s in hamsters
Symptoms and Effects	Sudden onset of fever, malaise, muscle pain, headache and conjunctivitis, followed by sore throat, vomiting, diarrhea, rash, and both internal and external bleeding (begins 5th day). Liver function may be abnormal and platelet function may be impaired.	Hemorrhagic syndrome, chills, sweating, exhaustion and stupor	Febrile illness, sometimes abdominal tenderness; rarely shock, ocular problems	Sudden onset of fever, headache, backache, vomiting, marked prostration, and delirium; small blisters form crusts which fall off 10 d to 40 d after first lesions appear; opportunistic infection	Sudden illness with malaise, spiking fevers, rigors, severe headache, photophobia and myalgias
Treatment	No specific treatment exists. Severe cases require intensive supportive care, as patients are frequently dehydrated and in need of intravenous fluids.	No specific therapy; supportive therapy essential	No studies, but IV ribavirin (30 mg/ kg/6 h for 4 d, then 7.5 mg/kg/8 h for 6 d) should be effective	Vaccinia immune globulin (VIG), and supportive therapy	Supportive treatments only
Potential as Biological Agent	High—actually weaponized by former Soviet Union biological program	Unknown	Difficulties with mosquitos as vectors	Possible, especially since routine smallpox vaccination programs have been eliminated world-wide (part of USSR offense bioprogram)	High—former US and USSR offensive biological programs weaponized both liquid and dry forms for aerosol distribution.

Table 3–6. Viral agents-Continued

Biological Agent/Disease	Yellow Fever Virus	Dengue Fever Virus	Ebola Virus	Congo-Crimean Hemorrhagic Fever Virus
Likely Method of Dissemination	Mosquito-borne	Mosquito-borne	1. Direct contact 2. Aerosol (BA)	Unknown
Transmissible Person to Person	No	No	Moderate	Yes
Incubation Period	3 d to 6 d	3 d to 15 d	4 d to 16 d	7 d to 12 d
Duration of Illness	2 wk	1 wk	Death between 7 d to 16 d	9 d to 12 d
Lethality	10 % to 20 % death in severe cases or full recovery after 2 d to 3 d	5 % average case fatality by producing shock and hemorrhage, leading to death	High for Zaire strain; moderate with Sudan	15 % to 20 %
Vaccine Efficacy (for aerosol exposure)/ Antitoxin	Vaccine available; confers immunity for >10 yr	Vaccine available	No vaccine	No vaccine available; prophylactic ribavirin may be effective
Symptoms and Effects	Sudden onset of chills, fever, prostration, aches, muscular pain, congestion, severe gastrointestinal disturbances, liver damage and jaundice; hemorrhage from skin and gums	Sudden onset of fever, chills, intense headache, pain behind eyes, joint and muscle pain, exhaustion and prostration	Mild febrile illness, then vomiting, diarrhea, rash, kidney and liver failure, internal and external hemorrhage (begins 5th day), and petechiae	Fever, easy bleeding, petechiae, hypotension and shock; flushing of face and chest, edema, vomiting, diarrhea
Treatment	No specific treatment; supportive treatment (bed rest and fluids) for even the mildest cases	No specific therapy; supportive therapy essential	No specific therapy; supportive therapy essential	No specific treatment
Potential as Biological Agent	High, if efficient dissemination device is employed	Unknown	Former Soviet Union	Unknown

Table 3−7. Rickettsiae

Biological Agent/Disease	Endemic Typhus	Epidemic Typhus	Q Fever	Rocky Mountain Spotted Fever
Likely Method of Dissemination	1. Contaminated feces 2. Infected insect larvae 3. Rat or flea bites	1. Contaminated feces 2. Infected insect larvae	1. Sabotage (food supply) 2. Aerosol	Infected wood ticks
Transmissible Person to Person	No	No	Rare	No
Incubation Period	6 d to 14 d	6 d to 15 d	14 d to 26 d	3 d to 14 d
Duration of Illness	Unknown	Unknown	Weeks	Unknown
Lethality	1 %, increasing in people >50 yr old	10 % to 40 % untreated; increases with age	Very low	15 % to 20 % untreated, (higher in adults); treated—death rare with specific therapy (tetracycline or chloramphenicol)
Vaccine Efficacy (for aerosol exposure)/ Antitoxin	Unknown	Vaccine confers protection of uncertain duration	94 % protection against 3500 LD_{50}s in guinea pigs	No vaccine
Symptoms and Effects	Sudden onset of headache, chills, prostration, fever, pain; maculae eruption on 5th day to 6th day on upper body, spreading to all but palms, soles, or face, but milder than epidemic form	Sudden onset of headache, chills, prostration, fever, pain; maculae eruption on 5th day to 6th day on upper body, spreading to all but palms, soles, or face	Mild symptoms (chills, headaches, fever, chest pains, perspiration, loss of appetite)	Fever and joint pain, muscular pain; skin rash that spreads rapidly from ankles and wrists to legs, arms, and chest; aversion to light
Treatment	Antibiotics (tetracycline and chloramphenicol); supportive treatment and prevention of secondary infections	Antibiotics (tetracycline and chloramphenicol); supportive treatment and prevention of secondary infections	Tetracycline (500 mg/6 h, 5 d to 7 d) or doxycycline (100 mg/12 h, 5 d to 7 d) also, combined Erthyromycin (500 mg/6 h) and rifampin (600 mg/d)	Antibiotics—tetracycline or chloramphenicol
Potential as Biological Agent	Uncertain—broad range of incubation (6 d to 14 d) period could cause infection of force deploying biological agent	Uncertain—broad range of incubation (6 d to 14 d) period could cause infection of force deploying biological agent	Highly infectious, is delivered in aerosol form. Dried agent is very stable; stable in aerosol form.	Unknown

Table 3–8. Biological toxins

Biological Agent/Disease	Botulinum Toxin	Staphylococcal enterotoxin B	Tricothecene mycotoxins	Ricin (Isolated from Castor Beans)	Saxitoxin
Likely Method of Dissemination	1. Aerosol 2. Sabotage (food and water)	1. Sabotage (food supply) 2. Aerosol	1. Aerosol 2. Sabotage	1. Aerosol 2. Sabotage (food and water)	Contaminated shellfish; in biological scenario, inhalation or toxic projectile
Transmissible Person to Person	No	No	No	No	No
Incubation Period	Variable (hours to days)	3 h to 12 h	2 h to 4 h	Hours to days	5 min to 1 h
Duration of Illness	Death in 24 h to 72 h; lasts months if not lethal	Hours	Days to months	Days—death within 10 d to 12 d for ingestion	Death in 2 h to 12 h
Lethality	5 % to 60 %, untreated <5 % treated	<1 %	Moderate	100 %, without treatment	High without respiratory support
Vaccine Efficacy (for aerosol exposure)/ Antitoxin	Botulism antitoxin (IND) Prophylaxis toxoid (IND) Toxolide	No vaccine	No vaccine	No vaccine	No vaccine
Symptoms and Effects	Ptosis; weakness, dizziness, dry mouth and throat, blurred vision and diplopia, flaccid paralysis	Sudden chills, fever, headache, myalgia, nonproductive cough, nausea, vomiting and diarrhea	Skin—pain, pruritis, redness and vesicles, sloughing of epidermis; respiratory—nose and throat pain, discharge, sneezing, coughing, chest pain, hemoptysis	Weakness, fever, cough, pulmonary edema, severe respiratory distress	Light headedness, tingling of extremities, visual disturbances, memory loss, respiratory distress, death
Treatment	Antitoxin with respiratory support (ventilation)	Pain relievers and cough suppressants for mild cases; for severe cases, may need mechanical breathing and fluid replenishment	No specific antidote or therapeutic regimen is available; supportive and symptomatic care	Oxygen, plus drugs to reduce inflammation and support cardiac and circulatory functions; if ingested, empty the stomach and intestines; replace lost fluids	Induce vomiting, provide respiratory care, including artificial respiration
Potential as Biological Agent	Not very toxic via aerosol route; extremely lethal if delivered orally. Since covert poisoning is indistinguishable from natural botulism, poisoning could have limited use	Moderate—could be used in food and limited amounts of water (for example, at salad bars); LD_{50} is sufficiently small to prevent detection	High—used in aerosol form ("yellow rain") in Laos, Kampuchea and Afghanistan (through 1981)	Has been used in 1978—Markov murder (see ref. 7). Included on prohibited Schedule I chemicals list for Chemical Weapons Convention; high potential for use in aerosol form	Moderate, aerosol form is highly toxic

4. OVERVIEW OF RESPIRATORY PROTECTION SYSTEMS

In the context of PPE, respiratory protection systems or respirators provide protection by preventing the inhalation of harmful airborne substances and/or an oxygen-deficient atmosphere. Although there are many forms of respirators, they generally fall into the following two classes: air-purifying respirators and atmosphere-supplying respirators.

The type of fit and the mode of operation can further subcategorize both classes. Each class of respirator may be tight-fitting or loose-fitting. Tight-fitting respirators include facemasks made of flexible molded rubber, silicone, neoprene, or other materials. Typical designs incorporate rubber or woven elastic head straps. Tight-fitting respirators are available in three basic configurations. The first, called a "quarter-mask," covers the mouth and nose, and the lower sealing surface rests between chin and mouth. A second type, the "half-mask," fits over the nose and under the chin. Half-masks are designed to seal more reliably than quarter-masks, so they are preferred for use against greater hazards. A third type, the "full-facepiece," covers from roughly the hairline to below the chin. Typically, they provide the greatest protection, usually seal most reliably, and provide eye protection as well.

Generally, loose-fitting respirators enclose at least the head. A variety of configurations include hoods, helmets, and blouses. A light flexible device covering only the head and neck, or head, neck, and shoulders, is called a hood. If rigid protective headgear is incorporated into the design, it is called a helmet. Blouses extend down to the waist and some have wrist-length sleeves. Since these respirators are not tight-fitting, it is important that sufficient air is provided to maintain a slight positive pressure inside the hood relative to the environment immediately outside. In this way, an outward flow of air from the respirator prevents contaminants from entering the wearers breathing zone.

4.1 Air-Purifying Respirators

Air-purifying respirators are devices that contain a filter, cartridge, or canister that removes specific air contaminants by passing the ambient air through the air-purifying element before it is inhaled by the wearer. Elements that remove particulates are called filters, while vapor- and gas-removing elements are called either chemical cartridges or canisters. These respirators do not supply oxygen and must only be used when the surrounding atmosphere contains sufficient oxygen to sustain life, and the air contaminant level is below the concentration limits of the air-purifying element.

Filters and canisters or cartridges are the functional portions of air-purifying respirators, and they can generally be removed and replaced once their effective life has expired. Exceptions are filtering facepiece respirators, commonly referred to as "disposable respirators," "dust masks," or "single-use respirators," which cannot be cleaned, disinfected, or recharged after use. Air-purifying respirators are grouped into three functional types: particulate removing, vapor and gas removing, and combination. These respirators may be nonpowered or powered.

1. Particulate-removing respirators are designed to reduce inhaled concentrations of harmful aerosols and dusts by filtering most of the contaminants from the inhaled air before they

enter the breathing zone of the wearer. Different types of filtration technologies include mechanical filters (high efficiency particulate air (HEPA), and ultra low penetration air (ULPA)), electrostatic filters (which incorporate electrostatic charges into the filter medium), and membrane technologies (which provide physically separate air particles based on their size and geometry).

2. Vapor- and gas-removing respirators use sorbent chemicals such as activated charcoal or catalysts to remove (adsorb and/or absorb) specific gases and vapors from ambient air before they can enter the breathing zone of the wearer.

3. Combination cartridges and canisters are available to protect against particulates, as well as vapors and gases. An example of a combined vapor separation and particulate separation technology is the C2A1 canister, part of the M40 protective mask. The C2A1 canister contains HEPA filter layered with tetraethylene diamine (ASZM-TEDA) activated carbon vapor filter.

Three examples of air-purifying respirators are shown in figure 4–1, figure 4–2, and figure 4–3.

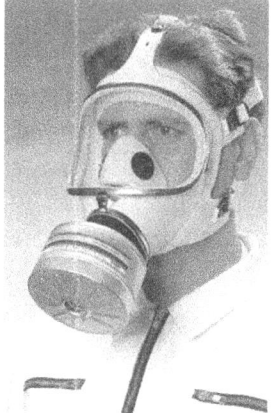

Figure 4–1. Panorama Nova Full Facepiece, Draeger Safety, Inc.

Figure 4–2. MSA Phalanx CBA/RCA Gas Mask, MSA

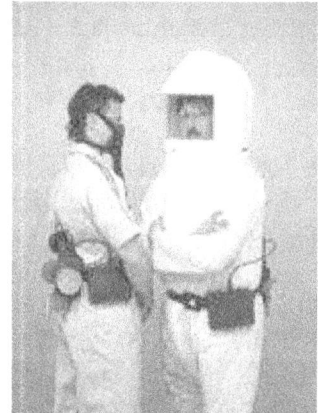

Figure 4–3. Survivair® Belt Mounted PAPR, Survivair, A Division of Bacou USA Safety, Inc.

4.1.1 Filtration Mechanisms

There are two types of particulate filters: absolute and nonabsolute. Absolute filters use screening to remove particles from the air; i.e., they exclude the particles that are larger than the pores. However, most respirator filters are nonabsolute filters, which means they contain pores that are larger than the particles to be removed. They use combinations of interception capture, sedimentation capture, inertial impaction capture, diffusion capture, and electrostatic capture to remove the particles. The exact combination of filtration mechanisms that comes into play depends upon the flowrate through the filter and the size of the particle. Brief descriptions of these filtration mechanisms follow:

1. Interception Capture. As the air streams approach a fiber lying perpendicular to their path, they split and compress in order to flow around the fiber and rejoin on the other side. If the center of a particle in these airstreams comes within one particle radius of the fiber, it encounters the fiber surface and is captured. As particle size increases, the probability of interception capture increases. The particles do not deviate from their original streamline in this mechanism.

2. Sedimentation Capture. Only large particles (2 µ and larger) are captured by sedimentation. Since this type of capture relies on gravity to pull particles from the airstream, flowrate through the filter must be low.

3. Inertial Impaction Capture. As the airstreams split and change direction suddenly to go around the fiber, particles with sufficient inertia cannot change direction sufficiently to avoid the fiber. Thus, they impact on the surface of the fiber. The size, density, speed, and shape of the particle determine its inertia.

4. Diffusion Capture. The motion of smaller particles is affected by air molecules colliding with them. The particles can then randomly cross the air stream and encounter the fiber as they pass. This random motion is dependent on particle size and the air temperature. As the particle size decreases and air temperature increases, the diffusive activity of the particle increases, which increases the probability of capture. Lower flow rate through the filter also increases the probability of capture because the particle spends more time in the area of the fiber.

5. Electrostatic Capture. In electrostatic capture, the target particles have a natural charge and the filter fibers are designed with the opposite charge. Therefore, the particles are attracted to the fibers. The electrostatic capture mechanism aids the other capture mechanisms, especially interception and diffusion.

4.1.2 Vapor and Gas Removal Mechanisms

Vapor-and gas-removing respirators normally remove the contaminant by interaction of its molecules with a granular, porous material, commonly called the sorbent. The general method by which the molecules are removed is called sorption. In addition to sorption, some respirators use catalysts, which react with the contaminant to produce a less toxic gas or vapor. Three removal mechanisms are used in vapor- and gas-removing respirators.

1. Adsorption retains the contaminant molecule on the surface of the sorbent granule by physical attraction. The intensity of the attraction varies with the type of sorbent and contaminant. Adsorption by physical attraction holds the adsorbed molecules weakly. However, if chemical forces are involved, as in the process called chemisorption, the bonds holding the molecules to the sorbent granules are much stronger and can be broken only with great difficulty.

   Activated charcoal is the most common adsorbent. It is used primarily to remove organic vapors. Activated charcoal also can be impregnated with other substances to make it more selective against specific gases and vapors. Examples are activated charcoal impregnated with iodine to remove mercury vapor, with metallic oxides to remove acid gases, and with salts of metals to remove ammonia gas. Other sorbents that could be used in vapor and gas removing respirators include molecular sieves, activated alumina, and silica gel.

2. Absorption may also be used to remove gases and vapors. Absorbents differ from adsorbents in that, although they are porous, they do not have as large a specific surface area. Absorption is also different because the gas or vapor molecules usually penetrate deeply into the molecular spaces throughout the sorbent and are held there chemically. Absorption may not be able to occur without prior adsorption on the surface of the particles. Furthermore, adsorption occurs instantaneously, whereas absorption is slower. Most absorbents are used for protection against acid gases. They include mixtures of sodium or potassium hydroxide with lime and/or caustic silicates.

3. Catalysts are substances that influence the rate of chemical reaction between other substances. A catalyst used in respirator cartridges and canisters is hopcalite, a mixture of porous granules of manganese and copper oxides that speeds the reaction between toxic carbon monoxide and oxygen to form carbon dioxide.

As applied to respirators, the vapor and gas removal processes described are essentially 100 % efficient until the sorbent's capacity to adsorb vapor and gas or catalyze their reaction is exhausted. Then the contaminant will pass completely through the sorbent and into the facepiece. This is in contrast to mechanical particulate-removing filters that become more efficient as matter collects on their surface and plugs the spaces between the fibers. This difference is important to remember. Water vapor reduces the effectiveness of some sorbents and increases that of others. For example, increasing moisture content of a sorbent designed to sorb acid gases may increase sorbent efficiency since most acid gases normally dissolve in water. Vapor- and gas-removing cartridges should be protected from the atmosphere while in storage.

4.1.3 Filter Efficiency and Efficiency Degradation

Filter efficiency indicates the percentage of particles the filter can remove from the air. Filter efficiency degradation is the lowering of filter efficiency or a reduction in the ability of the filter to remove particles. The Occupational Safety and Health Administration (OSHA) regulations establish nine classes of filters (three levels of filter efficiency, each with three categories of resistance to filter efficiency degradation). The three levels of filter efficiency are 95 %, 99 %, and 99.97 %. The three categories of resistance to filter efficiency degradation are labeled N (not for resistance to oil), R (for resistance to oil), and P (oil proof). The class of filter should be clearly marked on the filter, filter package, or respirator box. For example, a filter marked N95 would mean an N series filter that is at least 95 % efficient. Combination cartridges that include particulate filter elements carry a similar marking that pertains only to the particulate filter element.

4.1.4 Powered Air-Purifying Respirators (PAPR)

A PAPR uses a blower to force the ambient atmosphere through air purifying elements to the inlet covering. The covering may be a facepiece, helmet, hood, or blouse. PAPRs reduce the burden caused by drawing air through the filter element, therefore allowing the wearer to breathe easier.

PAPRs come in several different configurations. One configuration consists of the air-purifying element(s) attached to a small blower that is worn on the belt and is connected to the respiratory inlet covering by a flexible tube. The device is usually powered by a small battery, either mounted separately on the belt or as part of the blower. Some units are powered by an external DC or AC source. Another type of PAPR consists of the air-purifying element attached to a stationary blower, usually mounted on a vehicle, powered by a battery or an external power source and connected by a long flexible tube to the respiratory inlet covering. The third type of powered air-purifying respirator consists of a helmet or facepiece to which the air-purifying element and blower are attached. Only the battery is carried on the belt.

4.2 Atmosphere-Supplying Respirators

Atmosphere-supplying respirators provide clean breathing air from an uncontaminated source independent of the surrounding atmosphere instead of removing contaminants from the atmosphere. These respirators are grouped by the method that is used to supply air and the way in which the air supply is regulated. The three principle classes of atmosphere-supplying respirators are self-contained breathing apparatus, supplied-air respirators, and combination self-contained and supplied-air respirators.

1. Self-contained breathing apparatus (SCBA) is much like the apparatus a SCUBA diver or firefighter might use. Air is supplied from a compressed air cylinder, usually through a full-face mask, which is worn on the back. This generally allows greater movement than a supplied-air respirator; however, the air supply is limited.

2. Supplied-air respirators (SAR) (also called airline respirators) usually involve a facemask or hood connected to a stationary source of compressed air by a hose. The air is delivered continuously or intermittently in a sufficient volume to meet the wearer's breathing requirements. Obviously, the length of the hose connection, and the dangers of damage to or crimping of the hose, restrict the user.

3. Combination respirators have a small, auxiliary self-contained air supply that can be used if the primary supply (either by SCBA or SAR) is interrupted or fails.

4.2.1 Open-Circuit vs. Closed-Circuit SCBA

Self-contained breathing apparatus' (SCBAs) are available as open-circuit systems or closed-circuit systems. Open-circuit systems exhaust the exhaled air to the atmosphere instead of recirculating it. For example, an open-circuit SCBA utilizes a cylinder of compressed air that supplies air to a regulator, which reduces the pressure for delivery to the facepiece. The regulator is either mounted directly to the facepiece, or a flexible hose connects the regulator to a facepiece. The service life of the open-circuit SCBA is usually shorter than the closed-circuit SCBA because the compressed air cylinder must provide the total breathing volume requirements since there is no recirculation. Most open-circuit SCBA have a published useful period of 30 min to 60 min. However, these times may be cut in half with moderate to heavy workloads.

Another name for a closed-circuit SCBA is a rebreather device, indicative of its mode of operation. The breathing gas is rebreathed after the exhaled carbon dioxide has been removed (scrubbed) and the oxygen content restored by a compressed or liquid oxygen source or an oxygen-generating solid. These devices are designed primarily for 1 h to 4 h use in toxic and/or oxygen-deficient atmospheres. Figure 4–4, figure 4–5, and figure 4–6 illustrate three supplied air systems. The SCBA is the Draeger AirBoss PSS100 from Draeger Safety, Inc.; the rebreather is the Biomarine BioPak 240 Rebreather, from Biomarine, Inc., and the airline respirator is the ARAP/C and ARAP/E Airline Respirator, from International Safety Instruments.

4.2.2 Airflow Regulators

Regulators within atmosphere-supplying respirators provide three types of airflow: demand (negative pressure regulator), pressure demand (positive pressure regulator), and continuous flow.

Figure 4–4. Draeger AirBoss PSS100, Draeger Safety, Inc.

Figure 4–5. Biomarine BioPak 240 Rebreather, Biomarine, Inc.

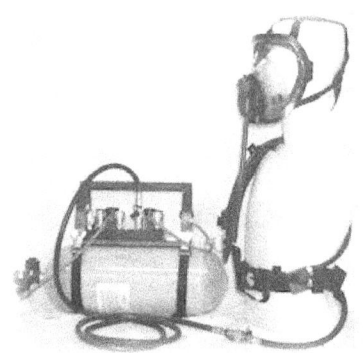

Figure 4–6. ARAP/C and ARAP/E Airline Respirator, International Safety Instruments

In a demand or negative pressure regulator, the air supply valve stays closed as long as there is positive pressure in the facepiece (during exhalation). Inhalation creates negative pressure in the facepiece, and the supply valve opens, allowing air into the facepiece. In other words, air flows into the facepiece only on "demand" by the wearer.

A pressure-demand or positive pressure regulator is very similar to a demand type except for a spring that tends to hold the supply valve slightly open, theoretically allowing continual air flow into the facepiece. However, all pressure-demand devices have a special exhalation valve that maintains positive backpressure in the facepiece and opens only when the pressure exceeds that value. This combination of modified regulator and special exhalation valve is designed to maintain positive pressure in the facepiece at all times. Under certain conditions, a momentary negative pressure may occur in the wearer's breathing zone, although the regulator still supplies additional air on "demand." Because of the positive pressure, any leakage should be outward; therefore, a pressure-demand system provides very good protection. Contrary to common belief, the pressure-demand SCBA has the same service time as a demand version of the same device, if it seals properly on the wearer's face. Any leakage increases air consumption and decreases service time.

Continuous-flow regulators maintain airflow at all times, rather than only on demand. In place of a demand or pressure-demand regulator, an airflow control valve or orifice partially controls the airflow. This means that by design, either the control valve cannot be closed completely, or a continually open bypass is provided to allow air to flow around the valve, maintaining positive flow rate. Continuous-flow regulators are used only with SARs and not SCBAs.

4.3 Escape Masks

Several models of escape masks are also included in this guide. Some escape masks are disposable and others can be reused but offer a minimum duration of protection. Figure 4–7 shows the disposable Parat NBC Escape Hood by Draeger, Inc., and figure 4–8 shows an emergency escape breathing apparatus, the Spiroscape Escape BA by Interspiro, Inc.

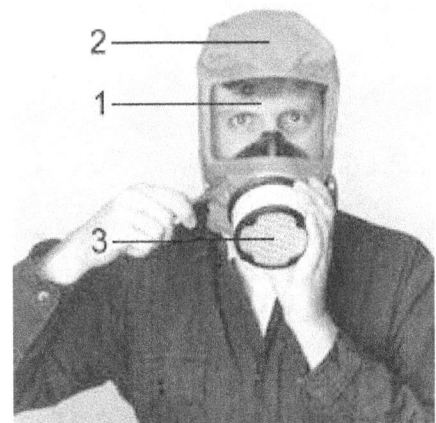

Figure 4–7. Parat NBC Escape Hood, Draeger Safety, Inc.

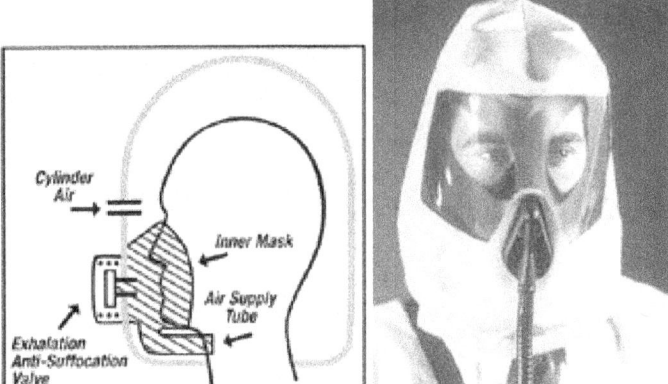

Figure 4–8. Spiroscape Escape BA, Interspiro Inc.

5. PERCUTANEOUS PROTECTION

Percutaneous protection or "chemical protective clothing" is designed to protect the skin from harmful exposure by either physical or chemical means. Chemical protective clothing can be classified by design and performance. Categorizing clothing by design means describing what areas of the body the clothing item is intended to protect. Categorizing clothing by performance means describing the relative level of protection the garments provide the wearer against liquid, aerosol, and vapor hazards.

5.1 Types of Chemical Protective Clothing

This guide groups chemical protective clothing into five principle classes: gas-tight encapsulating suits, liquid splash-protective suits, permeable protective suits, nonhazardous chemical protective clothing, and other protective apparel such as chemically resistant hoods, gloves, and boots.

5.1.1 Gas-Tight Encapsulating Suits

Gas-tight encapsulating suits provide a vapor-protective barrier that completely covers the wearer and their respirator. These suits are intended for response situations where no chemical contact (neither liquid nor vapor) is permissible. This type of suit is equivalent to the clothing required in EPA's Level A. Figure 5–1 and figure 5–2 illustrate an EPA Level A fully encapsulated suit and a Level A ensemble, respectively.

Figure 5–1. Tychem® BR EX Commander Level A Fully Encapsulating Suit, DuPont Tyvek® Protective Apparel

Figure 5–2. Tychem® TK EX Commander Brigade Level A Ensemble, NFPA 1991 certified, DuPont Tyvek® Protective Apparel

5.1.2 Liquid Splash-Protective Suits

Liquid splash-protective suits are available as nongas-tight encapsulating suits, coveralls, or two-piece overgarments. These types of garments are made of essentially impermeable materials that offer protection against liquid chemicals in the form of splashes, but not against continuous liquid contact or chemical vapors. By wearing liquid splash-protective clothing, the wearer risks potential exposure to chemical vapors or gases because this clothing does not offer gas-tight performance. At best, these garments will meet the EPA Level B needs. Examples of EPA Level B garments are shown in figure 5–3, figure 5–4, and figure 5–5.

Figure 5–3. Tychem® SL Utility Level B Fully Encapsulating Suit, DuPont Tyvek® Protective Apparel

Figure 5–4. Kappler Responder® Level B Coverall with attached hood, Kappler Safety Group

Figure 5–5. Lakeland Tyvek® QC Level B Coverall with collar, Lakeland Industries, Inc.

5.1.3 Permeable Protective Suits

Permeable protective suits are available as nongas-tight encapsulating suits, coveralls, or two-piece overgarments, as well as protective undergarments. These types of garments are made of fabric that is permeable or semi-permeable to most molecules but also chemically alters or physically removes certain toxic materials before they can reach the skin. These garments are typically used by the military and can be worn for extended periods in situations that present a limited exposure to hazardous vapors and gases. It is important to note that these garments are not designed to protect against many common industrial chemicals. An example of protective clothing that uses adsorptive technology is the Saratoga Joint Service Lightweight Integrated Suit (JSLIST), from Tex-Shield, Inc., shown in figure 5–6.

*Figure 5–6. Saratoga Joint Service Lightweight
Integrated Suit (JSLIST), Tex-Shield, Inc.*

5.1.4 Nonhazardous Chemical Protective Clothing

Nonhazardous chemical protective clothing include garments made of traditional textiles that allow vapors and liquids to pass through and, therefore, do not offer protection against highly toxic CB agents and TIMs. These garments are generally used to keep the wearer free of dusts, soils, stains, and electrostatic charge.

5.1.5 Other Protective Apparel

Other protective apparel includes ancillary clothing items and accessories that complete or supplement a particular protective ensemble (e.g., hoods, aprons, sleeves, gloves, boots and boot covers, and tape). These items are generally intended for use in situations where the physical contact with hazardous material is limited and the hazard is completely characterized.

5.2 Material Chemical Resistance

The protective fabric technology and the protective clothing design are the two components that provide necessary protection from percutaneous hazards of CB agents and TIMs. Ideally, the selected fabrics that make up chemical protective clothing must resist permeation, degradation, and penetration by the respective chemicals.

5.2.1 Permeation

Permeation is the process by which a chemical dissolves in or moves through a material on a molecular basis. The higher the "rate of permeation," the faster a particular chemical will move through a select material. In most cases, there will be no visible evidence of chemicals permeating a material. The rate of permeation can be influenced by several factors such as chemical concentration, material thickness, humidity, temperature, and pressure. Permeation "breakthrough time" is the most common result used to assess material chemical compatibility. The time it takes a chemical to permeate completely through a particular material under a set of standardized conditions is the breakthrough time. Breakthrough time is determined by applying a particular chemical on the exterior surface of a fabric and measuring the time it takes to detect the chemical on the inside surface. The breakthrough time gives some indication of how long a garment can be used before the chemical will permeate through the material.

5.2.2 Degradation

Degradation involves physical changes in a material as the result of chemical exposure, use, or ambient conditions (e.g., heat or sunlight). The most common observations of material degradation are discoloration, swelling, loss of physical strength, or deterioration.

5.2.3 Penetration

Penetration is the movement of chemicals through fabric joints or openings such as zippers, seams, pinholes, or imperfections in a protective clothing material.

5.3 Service Life

Some manufacturers of protective clothing provide a recommended service life for their suits and apparel. Ultimately, clothing item service life is a user decision, depending on the costs and risks associated with clothing decontamination and reuse. Protective clothing may be labeled as reusable (for multiple wearings) or disposable (for one-time use).

Descriptive distinctions between these types of clothing are both vague and complicated. Disposable clothing is generally lightweight and inexpensive. Reusable clothing is often more rugged and costly. Nevertheless, extensive contamination of any garment may render it unfit for reuse. The basis of this classification really depends on the costs involved in purchasing, maintaining, and reusing protective clothing versus the alternative of disposing the protective clothing following exposure. If a user can anticipate using a garment several times while still maintaining adequate protection, the suit becomes reusable.

5.4 Percutaneous Protection Technologies

Technologies for percutaneous protection include the materials and material treatments. Technologies are divided into permeable material treatments, permeable sorptive materials, engineered permeable materials, and impermeable materials.

5.4.1 Permeable Material Treatments

Permeable materials are traditional textiles that allow vapors and liquids to pass through and, therefore, do not offer protective properties against CB agents and TIMs. These materials, when used in combination with treatments and finishes, have enhanced protective capabilities.

Examples of treatment technologies include high surface tension technology, wicking technology, and electrostatic surface treatments. Treatments and finishes can be applied when the material is fabricated or when the garment is assembled. Permeable material treatments are further divided into high surface tension technologies (HSTT), wicking technologies, and electrostatic surface treatment technologies.

5.4.2 Permeable Sorptive Materials

Permeable sorptive materials provide protection from vapor-phase contaminants by trapping vapors as they pass through the fabric. However, these materials do not protect as well against aerosols and liquids. Permeable sorptive materials are subdivided into activated carbon and zeolites. Activated carbon, or activated charcoal, has been used historically for protection against chemical agents, but it has limited performance, especially in humid environments. Carbon can also sorb contaminants such as petroleum, oils, and lubricants (POLs). Zeolites can be either naturally occurring or synthetic. Synthetic zeolites, also called molecular sieves, can be engineered with reactive sites to tailor specificity.

5.4.3 Engineered Permeable Materials

Engineered permeable materials have been specifically engineered to restrict the penetration of toxic contaminants through the material but still allow water vapor transmission for evaporative cooling and personal comfort. Permeable sorptive technologies include semi-permeable membranes, carbon-loaded semi-permeable membranes, nanofiber membranes, and reactive material technologies. Semi-permeable membrane technology is probably the most familiar and is commercially recognized as *Gore-Tex™*, which uses an expanded polytetrafluoroethylene (PTFE) polymer film. The carbon-loaded semi-permeable membrane technology was most recently evaluated for use in the Joint Service Lightweight Integrated Suit Technology (JSLIST) program.

5.4.4 Impermeable Materials

Impermeable materials prevent permeation of aerosols, liquids, and vapors. This applies to exterior contaminated air as well as to moisture and vapor produced by the user, creating uncomfortable environments when used for personal protective items. Impermeable materials are categorized in three major groups: homogeneous materials, laminates, and composites. Butyl rubber (used for boots, gloves, and suits) is an example of a homogeneous material. Laminates are produced by bonding two or more layers of material together. Combinations of different materials allow for optimization of the laminate properties. Currently, this technology is used as a base material for the Self-Contained Toxicological Environmental Protective Overgarment (STEPO).

5.4.5 Some Commercial Product Names and Technologies

The following table lists the names of some commercial products that are used in producing certain kinds of personal protective clothing (e.g., gloves, aprons, vests, and suits). This list gives the name of the manufacturer, a brief description of the material, and examples of what kinds of personal protective clothing are made from these materials. For more complete descriptions of the products and their uses and limitations, users should consult their safety equipment supplier and/or the manufacturer.

Table 5–1. Trade names, manufacturers, and descriptions of commonly used materials

Trade Name	Manufacturer	Description
4H™	Safety 4, Inc.	Multi-layer laminate of polyethylene (PE) and ethylene-vinyl alcohol (EVOH [ISO 1043–1] or EVAL)—offers protection against exposure to many chemicals and mixtures.
Barricade™	DuPont	A chemical barrier fabric (multilayer laminate) that provides excellent chemical resistance.
Chemrel™	Chemron UK	Multi-layered film barrier composites, laminated onto a soft polypropylene substrate; encapsulated suits made from different Chemrel (TM) fabrics are available, providing protection against different chemicals and gases.
Kevlar™	DuPont	Aramid (aromatic polyamide) fiber—tough textile fiber used in protective clothing where resistance to cuts, heat, bullets or flying fragments is needed.
Nomex™	DuPont	High-temperature-resistant aramid (aromatic polyamide) fiber; resistant to a wide range of industrial chemicals and solvents.
Responder™	Life-Guard	Multi-film material designed to offer a high degree of permeation resistance to a broad range of chemicals; also used in Level A vapor protective suits (totally encapsulated chemical [TECP] suits).
Saranex™	Dow Chemical Company	Multi-layer coextruded film made from polyethylene (PE), polyvinylidene chloride (PVDC), and ethylene-vinyl acetate (EVA or EVAC [ISO 1043–1 abbrev.]). Used as a coating for protective clothing.
Silver Shield™	Siebe North Inc.	A laminate material that offers excellent protection against a wide range of chemicals and solvents but does not have good cut resistance. Can be used as an inner glove to enhance protection where cuts/mechanical damage are likely.
Teflon™	DuPont	Fluorocarbon polymers made from tetrafluoroethylene (TFE) or a mixture of tetrafluoroethylene and hexafluoropropylene. Has excellent chemical and thermal resistance but poor physical strength properties; is combined with other materials in protective clothing.
Trellchem™	Trelleborg Protective Products AB	Trade name of a range of chemical protective suits. All are made with a polyamide fabric coated with different materials for the outside and inside layers, offering protection against exposure to wide range of chemicals; some suits (HPS, VPS, TLU-A) meet NFPA flammability test criteria. Trellchem HPS (High Performance Suit)™—Viton™ and butyl rubber outside and a polymer barrier laminate inside. Trellchem VPS (Vapour Barrier Suit)™—chloroprene rubber outside and a polymer barrier laminate inside. Trellchem Super™—Viton™ and butyl rubber outside and inside. Trellchem Butyl™—butyl rubber outside and inside. Trellchem Light™—polyvinyl chloride (PVC) outside and inside. Trellchem TLU (Limited Use)™—polymer barrier laminate outside and inside. Trellchem TLU-A™—ensemble comprising an aluminized fiberglass fabric over-cover and a Trellchem TLU suit.
Tychem™	DuPont	Offers protection against exposure to wide range of chemicals and is more tear- and puncture-resistant than Barricade™ material.
Viton™	DuPont Dow Elastomers	Series of synthetic fluororubbers, elastomers based on polymers made from hexafluoropropylene, and vinylidene fluoride or vinyl fluoride; other fluorocarbons may be used in some Viton™ products.
Zetex™	Newtex	Clothing products are woven from highly texturized silica yarns—an alternative to asbestos for gloves, etc., for protection against heat, flames, and sparks.

6. PERSONAL PROTECTIVE EQUIPMENT SELECTION FACTORS

Section 6 provides a discussion of 12 selection factors that are recommended for consideration by the emergency first responder community when selecting and purchasing PPE (respiratory and percutaneous). These factors were compiled by a panel of experienced scientists and engineers who have multiple years of experience in PPE, domestic preparedness, and identification of emergency first responder needs. The factors have also been shared with the emergency first responder community in order to get their thoughts and comments.

It is anticipated that as additional input is received from the emergency first responder community, additional factors may be added or existing factors may be modified. These factors were developed so that PPE could be compared and contrasted in order to assist with the selection and purchase of the most appropriate equipment. *It is important to note that the evaluation conducted using the 12 selection factors was based solely upon vendor-supplied data and no independent evaluation of equipment was conducted in the development of this guide.* The vendor-supplied data can be found in its entirety in Volume IIa (respiratory), Volume IIb (percutaneous—protective garments), and Volume IIc (percutaneous—other apparel).

In addition to the selection factor information, the agency certifying the system for use (i.e., OSHA, National Institute for Occupational Safety and Health (NIOSH), NFPA, etc.), if any, and testing is also included as part of the evaluation table.

The results of the evaluation of the PPE against the 12 selection factors are provided in section 7 (respiratory), section 8 (percutaneous—protective garments), and section 9 (percutaneous—other apparel), respectively. The remainder of this section defines each of the selection factors. Details on the manner in which the selection factor was used to assess the equipment are presented in table 6–1 (respiratory), table 6–2 (percutaneous—protective garments), and table 6–3 (percutaneous—other apparel).

6.1 Chemical Warfare (CW) Agents Protection

This factor describes the ability of the equipment to protect from chemical agents. Chemical agents, when referred to in this guide, refer to nerve and blister agents only. Blood agents and choking agents are included within the list of TIMs. Nerve agents primarily consist of GB and VX. Other nerve agents include GA, GD, and GF. Blister agents are primarily limited to mustard (H). The blister agents considered in this guide include HD, HN, and L.

6.2 Biological Warfare (BW) Agents Protection

This factor describes the ability of the equipment to protect from biological agents. Biological agents considered for this guide include bacteria (i.e., Anthrax), rickettsia (i.e., Typhus), toxins (i.e., Botulinum Toxin), and viruses (i.e., Q Fever).

6.3 Toxic Industrial Materials (TIMs) Protection

This factor describes the ability of the equipment to protect from TIMs. TIMs considered in the development of this guide are discussed in section 3. Examples include ammonia, carbon monoxide, hydrogen cyanide, phosgene, and mineral acids (i.e., hydrochloric acid, sulfuric acid, nitric acid, etc.).

6.4 Duration of Protection

Duration of protection indicates the amount of time the equipment provides adequate protection. Since duration varies depending on the concentration of agent, type of agent, and environmental conditions, duration will be given with respect to specific conditions.

6.5 Environmental Conditions

This factor indicates whether the equipment is designed for use in all common outdoor weather conditions and climates (e.g., rain, snow, extreme temperatures, and humidity) or only under relatively controlled conditions.

6.6 Weight/Comfort

Weight/comfort is the total weight of the equipment/system and indicates how long the equipment can be worn with no effects. This should be considered in conjunction with the dexterity/mobility selection factor. Weight/comfort is considered for both respiratory protection and percutaneous protection.

6.7 Dexterity/Mobility (Ease of Use)

Dexterity/mobility refers to the ease of use and comfort of an individual while wearing the personal protective system. Ease of use, as well as donning and doffing information, is an important consideration for this selection factor.

6.8 Sizes Available

Sizes available refers to the variety of sizes available to the first responder community. There should be enough sizes to adequately fit most of the members of the response team, both male and female.

One-size-fits-all may be attractive for certain items but may not serve the responder community that is made up of diverse personnel. This selection factor is not considered for respiratory protection.

6.9 Visibility

Visibility indicates the percentage of unobstructed visibility the user has while wearing the protective gear. This selection factor is appropriate for respiratory equipment, fully encapsulated protective garments, and other protective apparel (hoods).

6.10 Launderability (Cleaning)

Launderability includes the laundering procedures that are safe for the item, including the number of times it can be laundered or cleaned and remain effective. Also, launderability includes any special procedures needed for specific components. This selection factor is appropriate for respiratory equipment accessories (straps, harnesses), fully encapsulated protective garments, and other protective apparel.

6.11 Training Requirements

Training requirements indicate the amount of instruction time required for the responder to become proficient in the operation of the instrument. For example, higher-end equipment such as SCBA and PAPR respirators require more in-depth training than an escape mask. Also, fully encapsulated garments may require specific donning and doffing procedures.

Continuous training or periodic recertification in the use of the equipment is considered with this selection factor.

6.12 Unit Cost

Unit cost is the cost of the PPE, including the cost of all support equipment and consumables. This factor, in conjunction with other selection factors, can help decide if the equipment will be deemed suitable for disposal after use, suitable for special uses only, or suitable for all uses.

Table 6-1. Selection factor key for personal protective equipment (respiratory)

August 2001

Symbol	Chemical Agents Protection	Biological Agents Protection	TIMs Protection	Protection Duration	Environmental Conditions	Weight/Comfort	Dexterity/Mobility (Ease of Use)	Visibility	Launderability	Training Requirements	Cost
●	Protects against all nerve and blister agents	Protects against all biological agents	Protects against all TIMs listed	Protects up to 2 h	Protects in all environments	Easily manageable, able to be worn for long periods with no effects	Not limiting	90 % to 100 % visibility	Able to be cleaned and reused greater than 50 times	Little to no training required	Less than or equal to $500 per unit
◕								75 % to 90 % visibility	Able to be cleaned and reused 25 to 50 times		
◑	Protects against some of the nerve and blister agents	Protects against some biological agents	Protects against multiple TIMs	Protects 30 min to 90 min	Protects in normal environments	Manageable, but unable to wear for more than 1 to 2 h at a time	Some loss of mobility, range of motion	50 % to 75 % visibility	Able to be cleaned and reused 5 to 50 times	Some training required, 4 h or more	Greater than $500 but less than $1000 per unit
◔									Not intended for reuse, but can be hand cleaned to remove dirt and dust		
○	Protects against none of the blister or nerve agents	Protects against no biological agents	Protects against none of the TIMs listed	Protects less than 30 min	Protects only in specific environments	Very heavy and cumbersome, unable to wear for prolonged periods	Very limiting	Less than 50 % visibility	Unable to be reused	Continuous training required with recertification every few months	Greater than or equal to $1000 per unit

The blank cells designate that the symbol is not applicable for the selection factor.
A duplicate of this table is provided for quick reference as Table 7-10.

42

Table 6-2. Selection factor key for percutaneous protective (garments)
August 2001

Symbol	Chemical Agents Protection	Biological Agents Protection	TIMs Protection	Protection Duration	Environmental Conditions	Weight/Comfort	Dexterity/Mobility (Ease of Use)	Sizes Available	Visibility	Launderability	Training Requirements	Cost (Gas Tight)	Cost (Not Gas Tight)	Cost (Coveralls)
●	Protects against all nerve and blister agents	Protects against all biological agents	Protects against all TIMs listed	Protects up to 2 h	Protects in all environments	Easily manageable, able to be worn for long periods with no effects	Not limiting	At least 5 sizes available	90% to 100% visibility	Able to be cleaned and reused greater than 50 times	Little to no training required	Less than or equal to $500 per unit	Less than or equal to $100 per unit	Less than or equal to $75 for single unit or $150 for bulk packaging
◕									75% to 90% visibility	Able to be cleaned and reused 25 to 50 times				
◑	Protects against some of the nerve and blister agents	Protects against some biological agents	Protects against multiple TIMs	Protects 30 min to 90 min	Protects in normal environments	Manageable, but unable to wear for more than 1 h to 2 h at a time	Some loss of mobility, range of motion	At least 4 sizes available	50% to 75% visibility	Able to be cleaned and reused 5 to 50 times	Some training required, 4 h or more	Greater than $500 but less than $1000 per unit	Greater than $100 but less than $500 per unit	Greater than $75 (single unit) or $150 (bulk) but less than $300 for single item or bulk packaging
◔										Not intended for reuse, but can be hand cleaned to remove dirt and dust				
○	Protects against none of the blister or nerve agents	Protects against no biological agents	Protects against none of the TIMs listed	Protects less than 30 min	Protects only in specific environments	Very heavy and cumbersome, unable to wear for prolonged periods	Very limiting	One size fits all	Less than 50% visibility	Unable to be reused	Continuous training required with recertification every few months	Greater than or equal to $1000 per unit	Greater than or equal to $500 per unit	Greater than or equal to $300 for single unit or bulk packaging

The blank cells designate that the symbol is not applicable for the selection factor.
A duplicate of this table is provided for quick reference as Table 8-9.

Table 6-3. Selection factor key for percutaneous protective equipment (apparel)
August 2001

Symbol	Chemical Agents Protection	Biological Agents Protection	TIMs Protection	Duration of Protection	Environmental Conditions	Weight/Comfort	Dexterity/Mobility (Ease of Use)	Sizes Available Hoods and Aprons	Sizes Available Garments	Visibility	Launderability	Training Requirements	Cost (Hoods)	Cost (Foot Protection)	Cost (Hand and Arm Protection)	Cost (Other)
● (full)	Protects against all nerve and blister agents	Protects against all biological agents	Protects against all TIMs listed	Protects up to 2 h	Protects in all environments	Easily manageable, able to be worn for long periods with no effects	Not limiting	One size fits all	Many available sizes	90 % to 100 % visibility	Able to be cleaned and reused greater than 50 times	Little to no training required	Less than or equal to $500 per unit	Less than or equal to $100 per unit	Less than or equal to $75 for single unit or $150 for bulk packaging	Less than or equal to $75 for single unit or $150 for bulk packaging
◕ (3/4)										75 % to 90 % visibility						
◑ (1/2)	Protects against some of the nerve and blister agents	Protects against some biological agents	Protects against multiple TIMs	Protects 30 min to 90 min	Protects in normal environments	Manageable, but unable to wear for more than 1 h to 2 h at a time	Some loss of mobility, range of motion		Small, medium, and large	50 % to 75 % visibility	Able to be cleaned and reused 5 to 50 times	Some training required, 4 h or more	Greater than $500 but less than $1000 per unit	Greater than $100 but less than $500 per unit	Greater than $75 (single unit) or $150 (bulk) but less than $300 for single item or bulk packaging	Greater than $75 (single unit) or $150 (bulk) but less than $300 for single item or bulk packaging
◔ (1/4)											Not intended for reuse, but can be hand cleaned to remove dirt and dust					
○ (empty)	Protects against none of the blister or nerve agents	Protects against no biological agents	Protects against none of the TIMs listed	Protects less than 30 min	Protects only in specific environments	Very heavy and cumbersome, unable to wear for prolonged periods	Very limiting	Numerous sizes, requires fit test	One size fits all	Less than 50 % visibility	Unable to be reused	Continuous training required with recertification every few months	Greater than or equal to $1000 per unit	Greater than or equal to $500 per unit	Greater than or equal to $300 for single unit or bulk packaging	Greater than or equal to $300 for single unit or bulk packaging

The blank cells designate that the symbol is not applicable for the selection factor.
A duplicate of this table is provided for quick reference as Table 9-11.

7. EVALUATION OF RESPIRATORY PROTECTIVE EQUIPMENT

The market survey (refer to sec. 2.0 of Vol. IIa) conducted for CB agent and TIM personal protective equipment identified 69 different respiratory protection items. The details of the market survey, including data on each item, are provided in Volume IIa of this guide. This section documents the results of evaluating each of the respiratory protection items versus the 12 selection factors provided in section 6 of this volume. Section 7.1 defines the types of respiratory equipment and section 7.2 discusses the evaluation results.

7.1 Respiratory Protection

In order to display the evaluation results in a meaningful format, the respiratory protection equipment were grouped into two primary categories (air purifying and atmosphere supplying) and then further subcategorized by the mode of operation and type of fit of the equipment.

7.1.1 Air-Purifying Respirators

Air-purifying respirators contain a filter, cartridge, or canister that removes specific air contaminants by passing air from the surrounding atmospheric through the air-purifying element. Air purifying respirators may be nonpowered or powered.

- **Masks** are nonpowered and use the breathing action of the wearer to draw air through the filter element.

- **Powered air-purifying respirators (PAPRs)** use blowers to force ambient atmosphere through the air purifying elements.

7.1.2 Atmosphere-Supplying Respirators

Atmosphere-supplying respirators provide air from a source independent of the surrounding atmosphere rather than removing contaminants from the atmosphere. Level A and Level B configurations require atmosphere-supplying respirators that produce positive pressure within the suit.

- A **self-contained breathing apparatus (SCBA)** gets air from a compressed cylinder, usually through a half-mask.

- A **rebreather** is a closed circuit SCBA. The exhaled air is rebreathed after it has been passed over a scrubber to remove carbon dioxide and restore oxygen.

- **Airline respirators or supplied air respirators (SARs)** use supplied-air that is connected by a hose to a stationary source of compressed breathing air. Some respirators can be configured as either a SCBA or a SAR.

7.1.3 Escape Masks

Escape masks are special purpose respiratory protection devices. They are for emergency use only. They are designed to provide short duration respiratory protection, enabling the wearer to escape from an area that has developed a respiratory hazard. These devices may be either air-purifying or atmosphere-supplying respirators.

7.2 Evaluation Results

The evaluation results for the respiratory protective equipment are presented in tabular format for the 69 pieces of equipment identified at the time this guide was written. A table is presented for each of the identified categories. Each table includes the specific equipment and the symbol that corresponds to how the equipment item was characterized based upon each of the selection factor definitions. The acronym "TBD" is displayed in the appropriate cell if data were not available to characterize a specific selection factor. The acronym "NA" is displayed in the appropriate cell if the data were not applicable for a piece of equipment. The results of categorizing the percutaneous protective garments are presented in table 7–1.

Table 7–1. Respiratory protection equipment

Respiratory Equipment	Respiratory Protective Equipment		
	Air Purifying	Supplied Air	Total
Mask	29		29
PAPR	12		12
SCBA		10	10
SCBA/Rebreather		3	3
Airline		5	5
SCBA/Airline		3	3
Escape Mask	3	4	7
Total	**44**	**25**	**69**

Table 7-2 provides the table number and associated table pages for each of the usage categories.

Table 7–2. Evaluation results reference table

Table Name	Table Number	Page(s)
Respiratory protection (masks)	7–3	48–50
Respiratory protection (PAPR)	7–4	51–52
Respiratory protection (SCBA)	7–5	53
Respiratory protection (SCBA/rebreather)	7–6	54
Respiratory protection (airline respirator)	7–7	55
Respiratory protection (SCBA/airline respirator)	7–8	56
Respiratory protection (escape masks)	7–9	57
Selection factor key for personal protection equipment (respiratory)	7–10	58

7.2.1 Air-Purifying Respirators

There were 44 air-purifying respirators identified in the development of this guide. These respirators were further divided into two subcategories, nonpowered masks and PAPRs. There were 29 nonpowered masks and 12 PAPRs. Three devices fall into the categories of escape masks. Table 7–3 and table 7–4 detail the evaluation results for these two air-purifying respirator subcategories, respectively.

7.2.2 Atmosphere-Supplying Respirators

There were 25 atmosphere-supplying respirators identified in the development of this guide. These atmosphere-supplying respirators were further divided into subcategories identifying the air supply (self contained and stationary source). The major atmosphere-supplying respirator category was the SCBA. There were 16 respirators identified as SCBA and five respirators with stationary air supply. The 16 SCBAs were further divided into SCBA (ten items), SCBA/ rebreather (three items), and SCBA/airline (three items). Table 7–5, table 7–6, table 7–7, and table 7–8 detail the evaluation results for SCBA, SCBA/rebreather, airline, and SCBA/airline, respectively.

7.2.3 Escape Masks

There were seven escape masks included in this guide, three air-purifying respirators, and four atmosphere-supplying respirators. Table 7–9 details the evaluation results for this category.

Table 7-3. Respiratory protection (masks)
August 2001

ID #	Equipment Name	Certifications/Regulations*	Chemical Agents Protection	Biological Agents Protection	TIMs Protection	Protection Duration	Environmental Conditions	Weight/Comfort	Dexterity/Mobility (Ease of Use)	Visibility	Launderability	Training Requirements	Cost
1	Avon CT12 Special Forces Respirator	NIOSH, OSHA	●	◐	TBD	●	◐	●	●	●	●	●	TBD
2	NBC FM12 Respirator	NIOSH, OSHA	●	◐	TBD	●	◐	●	●	●	●	●	TBD
3	NBC SF10 Respirator	NIOSH, OSHA	●	◐	TBD	●	◐	●	●	●	●	●	TBD
16	BG-4 w/Mask	NIOSH/MSHA	TBD	TBD	●	◐	◐	TBD	TBD	TBD	○	TBD	TBD
18	Panorama Nova Full Facepiece	NIOSH, NFPA, OSHA	●	◐	TBD	●	◐	●	◐	●	●	●	●
20	Kareta M Mask	NIOSH	TBD	TBD	TBD	TBD	TBD	TBD	TBD	TBD	TBD	TBD	●
25	M40 Series Gas Mask	AR 70-71; Canister Mount—NATO Standard	●	◐	◐	TBD	●	◐	TBD	TBD	TBD	TBD	●
26	M42 Series Gas Mask	AR 70-71; Canister Mount—NATO Standard	●	◐	◐	TBD	●	◐	TBD	TBD	TBD	TBD	●
30	INTERSPIRO Respirator	TBD	TBD	TBD	TBD	TBD	TBD	TBD	TBD	TBD	TBD	TBD	TBD
31	C4 Gas Mask	Canadian Department of National Defense	●	●	●	●	●	●	●	●	●	●	●
34	Magnum 4000 PS, with Full Facemask	TBD	NA	NA	●	◐	●	●	◐	●	●	●	●

'NA' - the specific selection factor is not applicable for the piece of equipment.
'TBD' (to be determined) - there is currently no data available to support that selection factor.
See Table 7-10 for selection factor definitions.
* See Appendix B, References, number eight.

Table 7-3. Respiratory protection (masks)-Continued
August 2001

ID #	Equipment Name	Certifications/Regulations*	Chemical Agents Protection	Biological Agents Protection	TIMs Protection	Protection Duration	Environmental Conditions	Weight/Comfort	Dexterity/Mobility (Ease of Use)	Visibility	Launderability	Training Requirements	Cost
53	3M™ 6000 Series Full Facepiece Respirators	OSHA 1910.134, NIOSH-approved when used with AEP3 cartridge (4240-01-323-3530)	TBD	TBD	◐	TBD	TBD	●	●	◐	TBD	◐	●
54	3M™ 6000 Series Full Facepiece Respirator	OSHA 1910.134, NIOSH-approved when used with AEP3 cartridge (4240-01-323-3530)	◐	◐	◐	TBD	TBD	●	●	◐	TBD	◐	●
55	3M™ 7800S-BA Full Facepiece Respirators	TBD	◐	◐	◐	TBD	TBD	TBD	TBD	TBD	◐	TBD	TBD
60	3M™ Full Facepiece FR-M40, Military-Style	NIOSH Cartridge manufactured in accordance with U.S. MIL-C51560 (EA) and EA-C-1704	●	TBD	●	TBD	TBD	TBD	TBD	TBD	TBD	TBD	TBD
63	PAN1 Dual Cartridge Full Face Respirator	NIOSH	●	●	◐	TBD	◐	●	●	◐	●	●	●
64	PAN2 Single Filter Canister	EN-136 Approved Respirator	●	●	◐	TBD	◐	●	●	◐	●	●	●
65	Model 4A1 NBC Respirator	TBD	●	●	◐	TBD	●	●	●	◐	●	●	TBD
66	M15-A30 NBC Respirator	NIOSH	●	●	◐	TBD	●	●	●	◐	●	●	TBD

'NA' - the specific selection factor is not applicable for the piece of equipment.
'TBD' (to be determined) - there is currently no data available to support that selection factor.
See Table 7-10 for selection factor definitions.
* See Appendix B, References, number eight.

Table 7-3. Respiratory protection (masks)-Continued
August 2001

ID #	Equipment Name	Certifications/Regulations*	Chemical Agents Protection	Biological Agents Protection	TIMs Protection	Protection Duration	Environmental Conditions	Weight/Comfort	Dexterity/Mobility (Ease of Use)	Visibility	Launderability	Training Requirements	Cost
35	Magnum 4500 P3, with Full Facemask	TBD	NA	NA	◐	●	◐	●	◐	◐	●	●	●
36	Magnum 8000 P3, with Full Facemask	TBD	NA	NA	◐	●	◐	●	◐	◐	●	●	●
37	Magnum 8500 P3, with Full Facemask	TBD	NA	NA	◐	●	◐	●	◐	◐	●	●	●
39	M95 Respirator NBC Protective Respirator	TBD	●	●	●	◐	●	●	TBD	TBD	●	●	●
40	MSA Advantage 1000 CBA/RCA Full-Face Respirator	NIOSH/MSHA no. TC-14G-0235	●	◐	●	◐	●	●	◐	●	●	●	●
41	MSA Advantage 1000 with GME-P100 cartridges	NIOSH-approved for all industrial chemicals	●	●	●	◐	●	●	◐	●	●	●	●
42	MSA Millennium Chemical-Biological Mask	NIOSH evaluating	●	●	TBD	◐	●	●	◐	●	●	●	●
45	MSA Phalanx CBA/RCA Gas Mask	NIOSH No. TC-14G-0236	●	◐	●	◐	●	●	◐	●	●	●	●
48	MSA Ultra-Twin® Respirators	TBD	TBD	TBD	TBD	TBD	TBD	●	TBD	TBD	TBD	TBD	TBD
49	MSA MCU-2/P and MCU-2A/P Series	TBD	●	●	TBD	TBD	●	◐	●	TBD	TBD	TBD	TBD

'NA' - the specific selection factor is not applicable for the piece of equipment.

'TBD' (to be determined) - there is currently no data available to support that selection factor.

See Table 7-10 for selection factor definitions.

* See Appendix B, References, number eight.

Table 7-4. Respiratory protection (PAPR)
August 2001

ID #	Equipment Name	Certifications/Regulations*	Chemical Agents Protection	Biological Agents Protection	TIMs Protection	Protection Duration	Environmental Conditions	Weight/Comfort	Dexterity/Mobility (Ease of Use)	Visibility	Launderability	Training Requirements	Cost
12	Sabre Tornado® Respiratory System (PAPR)	NIOSH regulations 42 CFR 84	TBD	TBD	TBD	TBD	TBD	TBD	TBD	TBD	TBD	TBD	TBD
22	PP Mask with ABP3/US canister	Positive pressure: NIOSH-approved (French version EN-approved) Negative pressure: EN-approved in French version	●	●	●	●	●	●	◐	◐	●	●	●
23	PAPR system	NIOSH-approved (French version EN-approved)	●	●	●	●	●	●	◐	●	●	●	◐
43	MSA OptimAir® MM 2K PAPR	NIOSH approval varies depending on facepiece or hood style	◐	◐	●	●	●	●	◐	●	●	●	●
44	MSA OptimAir® 6A PAPR with CBA/RCA OptiFilter Cartridges	NIOSH and MSHA	●	●	◐	●	●	●	◐	●	●	●	●
51	3M™ Breathe Easy™ 7 RRPAS™ Respirator	NIOSH, OSHA 1910.134, NIOSH-approved for certain chemicals and as high efficiency filter when used with AEP3 cartridge (4240-01-323-3530)	TBD	TBD	●	TBD	◐	●	◐	TBD	TBD	◐	◐
52	3M™ Breathe Easy™ Powered Air Purifying Respirator System	OSHA 1910.134, NIOSH-approved for certain chemicals when used with AEP3 cartridge	TBD	TBD	TBD	TBD	●	●	◐	TBD	◐	TBD	◐
57	3M™ Bell-Mounted PAPR	TBD	TBD	TBD	TBD	TBD	●	●	TBD	◐	●	TBD	TBD

'NA' - the specific selection factor is not applicable for the piece of equipment.
'TBD' (to be determined) - there is currently no data available to support that selection factor.
See Table 7-10 for selection factor definitions.
* See Appendix B, References, number eight.

51

Table 7-4. Respiratory protection (PAPR)-Continued
August 2001

ID #	Equipment Name	Certifications/Regulations*	Chemical agents Protection	Biological agents Protection	TIMs Protection	Protection Duration	Environmental Conditions	Weight/Comfort	Dexterity/Mobility (Ease of Use)	Visibility	Launderability	Training Requirements	Cost
58	3M™ GVP Belt-Mounted Powered Air Purifying Respirator	OSHA 1910.134, NIOSH-approved for certain organic vapors, acid gases and as a high efficiency filter when used with the GVP-443 cartridge (4240-01-394-6336)	TBD	TBD	TBD	TBD	●	●	◐	TBD	◐	◐	◐
62	Scott C420 Vaniflo™ PAPR	NFPA, OSHA, NIOSH, DOJ Foundation	TBD	TBD	TBD	TBD	TBD	TBD	TBD	TBD	TBD	TBD	TBD
67	SE400 Fan Supplied, Positive Pressure Respirator (FPBR)	NIOSH, CE	◐	◐	●	●	●	●	◐	NA	●	●	○
69	Survivair™ Belt Mounted PAPR	NIOSH Approval No. TC-23C-1053; ANSI/UL 913 standard for use in Class 1, Division 1, Groups A, B, C, and D hazards	TBD	TBD	TBD	TBD	●	●	TBD	TBD	TBD	TBD	TBD

'NA' - the specific selection factor is not applicable for the piece of equipment.
'TBD' (to be determined) - there is currently no data available to support that selection factor.
See Table 7-10 for selection factor definitions.
* See Appendix B, References, number eight.

Table 7-5. Respiratory protection (SCBA)
August 2001

ID #	Equipment Name	Certifications/Regulations*	Chemical Agents Protection	Biological Agents Protection	TIMS Protection	Protection Duration	Environmental Conditions	Weight/Comfort	Dexterity/Mobility (Ease of Use)	Visibility	Launderability	Training Requirements	Cost
4	Avon NBC-SCBA-Option	NIOSH, OSHA	●	●	◐	●	TBD	●	●	●	●	TBD	TBD
5	NBC CoolAir SCBA	TBD	●	●	●	●	◐	●	TBD	TBD	●	○	○
6	SuperCritical Air Mobility Pack (SCAMP®) Self Contained Breathing Apparatus (SCBA)	TBD	●	●	◐	TBD	◐	◐	TBD	TBD	●	○	○
14	AirBoss PSS100 with Flashing Gauge or with Sentinel I	NIOSH, MSHA, NFPA 1981/1997 edition, IPASS II or Sentinel compliant to NFPA 1982/1998 edition	●	●	◐	●	◐	◔	TBD	●	●	○	○
15	AirBoss Evolution with Flashing Gauge or with Sentinel	NIOSH, MSHA, NFPA 1981/1997 edition, IPASS II or Sentinel compliant to NFPA 1982/1998 edition	●	●	◐	●	◐	◔	TBD	●	●	○	○
17	ProAir Evolution	NIOSH	●	●	●	●	●	●	◐	●	●	○	
28	Viking Digital SCBA	NIOSH-approved	○	◐	◐	◐	●	●	●	●	◐	○	
50	MSA MMR Xtreme® Air Mask	ANSI/NFPA-1981 Standard for Open-circuit SCBA, 1997 Edition, NIOSH	TBD	TBD	TBD	TBD	TBD	TBD	TBD	TBD	TBD	TBD	
56	3M™ SCBAG Self-Contained Breathing Apparatus	OSHA 1910.134, NIOSH-approved in several configurations	●	●	◐	TBD	◐	◐	◐	TBD	◐	○	
68	Survivair™ Cougar SCBA	TBD	TBD	TBD	◐	◐	●	●	◐	TBD	TBD	TBD	TBD

'NA' - the specific selection factor is not applicable for the piece of equipment.
'TBD' (to be determined) - there is currently no data available to support that selection factor.
See Table 7-10 for selection factor definitions.
* See Appendix B, References, number eight.

Table 7-6. Respiratory protection (SCBA/rebreather)
August 2001

ID #	Equipment Name	Certifications/Regulations*	Chemical Agents Protection	Biological Agents Protection	TIMs Protection	Protection Duration	Environmental Conditions	Weight/Comfort	Dexterity/Mobility (Ease of Use)	Visibility	Launderability	Training Requirements	Cost
7	Biomarine BioPak 60 Rebreather	NIOSH/MSHA Certification TC-13F-371 and TC-13F-372	TBD	TBD	◐	●	●	●	◐	◐	NA	◐	○
8	Biomarine BioPak 240 Rebreather	NIOSH/MSHA Certification TC-13F-185 and TC-13F-206	◐	TBD	●	●	●	◐	◐	◐	NA	◐	○
32	Lirpac II-Rebreather	NIOSH/MSHA #TC-13F-233; DOT regulations for transporting full cylinders	●	●	●	●	●	●	◐	●	●	○	○

'NA' - the specific selection factor is not applicable for the piece of equipment.
'TBD' (to be determined) - there is currently no data available to support that selection factor.
See Table 7-10 for selection factor definitions.
* See Appendix B, References, number eight.

54

Table 7-7. Respiratory protection (airline respirator)
August 2001

ID #	Equipment Name	Certification/Regulations*	Chemical Agents Protection	Biological Agents Protection	TIMs Protection	Protection Duration	Environmental Conditions	Weight/Comfort	Dexterity/Mobility (Ease of Use)	Visibility	Launderability	Training Requirements	Unit Cost
9	Bullard CC20 Series Airline Respirator	MSHA/NIOSH, ASTM F739	TBD	TBD	TBD	●	TBD	●	●	TBD	TBD	TBD	TBD
11	Sabre Tornado® Respiratory System (Airline)	TBD	TBD	TBD	TBD	TBD	TBD	●	TBD	TBD	TBD	TBD	TBD
27	ARAP/C and ARAP/E Airline Respirators	NIOSH-approved Type C respirators	TBD	TBD	○	◐	●	●	●	●	●	●	TBD
33	Easiflow Plus Full Facemask Respirator and Filters	TBD	NA	NA	●	◐	●	●	◐	●	●	●	●
38	9 mtr Unpowered Fresh-Air Hose System	TBD	NA	NA	●	◐	●	●	◐	●	●	●	●

'NA' - the specific selection factor is not applicable for the piece of equipment.
'TBD' (to be determined) - there is currently no data available to support that selection factor.
See Table 7-10 for selection factor definitions.
* See Appendix B, References, number eight.

Table 7-8. Respiratory protection (SCBA/airline respirator)
August 2001

ID #	Equipment Name	Certifications/Regulations*	Chemical Agents Protection	Biological Agents Protection	TIMS Protection	Protection Duration	Environmental Conditions	Weight/Comfort	Dexterity/Mobility (Ease of Use)	Visibility	Launderability	Training Requirements	Cost
46	MSA PremAire™ XV Supplied Air Respirator	NIOSH/MSHA for entry and escape from IDLH atmospheres	TBD	◗	○	TBD	TBD	TBD	TBD	TBD	TBD	TBD	TBD
47	MSA RescueAire™ II Portable Air-Supply System	NIOSH/MSHA for entry and escape from IDLH atmospheres	TBD	◗	TBD	TBD	TBD	TBD	TBD	TBD	TBD	TBD	TBD
61	Scott AV 2000 AV-2000® Facepiece	TBD	TBD	TBD	TBD	TBD	TBD	TBD	TBD	TBD	TBD	TBD	TBD

'NA' - the specific selection factor is not applicable for the piece of equipment.
'TBD' (to be determined) - there is currently no data available to support that selection factor.
See Table 7-10 for selection factor definitions.
* See Appendix B, References, number eight.

56

Table 7-9. Respiratory protection (escape masks)
August 2001

ID #	Equipment Name	Certifications/Regulations*	Chemical Agents Protection	Biological Agents Protection	TIMs Protection	Protection Duration	Environmental Conditions	Weight/Comfort	Dexterity/Mobility (Ease of Use)	Visibility	Launderability	Training Requirements	Cost
10	Bullard Spectrum-PDE Pressure Demand Respirator with ESCBA	TBD	TBD	TBD	TBD	TBD	TBD	●	TBD	TBD	TBD	TBD	TBD
13	SR-100, 60 Minute ESCBA	NIOSH/MSHA certification (TC-13F-239). Meets CFR 30, part 75-1714 and CFR 29, 1910,146 Appendix E.	●	TBD	◐	◐	◐	◐	TBD	●	●	●	◐
19	Defend Air	TBD	●	◐	○	●	●	●	◕	○	○	●	●
21	Duram Emergency Escape Respirator	TBD	●	●	TBD	TBD	●	●	○	○	○	●	●
24	EVATOX Adult Escape Hood US	EN-approved (French version EN-approved)	◐	◐	◐	◐	●	●	●	●	○	●	●
29	Interspiro Spiroscape Escape BA	CE or NIOSH certification	TBD	TBD	○	TBD	●	●	◐	●	TBD	TBD	TBD
59	3M™ Escort Combination ESCBA/Supplied Air Respirator	OSHA 1910.134, NIOSH-approved in several configurations	TBD	TBD	TBD	TBD	●	●	◐	TBD	TBD	◐	◐

'NA' - the specific selection factor is not applicable for the piece of equipment.
'TBD' (to be determined) - there is currently no data available to support that selection factor.
See Table 7-10 for selection factor definitions.
* See Appendix B, References, number eight.

57

Table 7-10. Selection factor key for personal protective equipment (respiratory)
August 2001

Symbol	Chemical Agents Protection	Biological Agents Protection	TIMs Protection	Protection Duration	Environmental Conditions	Weight/Comfort	Dexterity/Mobility (Ease of Use)	Visibility	Launderability	Training Requirements	Cost
●	Protects against all nerve and blister agents	Protects against all biological agents	Protects against all TIMs listed	Protects up to 2 h	Protects in all environments	Easily manageable, able to be worn for long periods with no effects	Not limiting	90 % to 100 % visibility	Able to be cleaned and reused greater than 50 times	Little to no training required	Less than or equal to $500 per unit
◕								75 % to 90 % visibility	Able to be cleaned and reused 25 to 50 times		
◑	Protects against some of the nerve and blister agents	Protects against some biological agents	Protects against multiple TIMs	Protects 30 min to 90 min	Protects in normal environments	Manageable, but unable to wear for more than 1 h to 2 h at a time	Some loss of mobility, range of motion	50 % to 75 % visibility	Able to be cleaned and reused 5 to 50 times	Some training required, 4 h or more	Greater than $500 but less than $1000 per unit
◔									Not intended for reuse, but can be hand cleaned to remove dirt and dust		
○	Protects against none of the blister or nerve agents	Protects against no biological agents	Protects against none of the TIMs listed	Protects less than 30 min	Protects only in specific environments	Very heavy and cumbersome, unable to wear for prolonged periods	Very limiting	Less than 50 % visibility	Unable to be reused	Continuous training required with recertification every few months	Greater than or equal to $1000 per unit

The blank cells designate that the symbol is not applicable for the selection factor.

8. EVALUATION OF PERCUTANEOUS PROTECTION (GARMENTS)

The market survey (refer to sec. 2.0 of Vol. IIb) conducted for CB agent and TIM personal protective equipment identified 180 different protective garments. The details of the market survey, including data on each item, are provided in Volume IIb of this guide. This section documents the results of evaluating each percutaneous protective garment versus the 12 selection factors provided in section 6 of this volume. Section 8.1 defines the levels of protection of the garments and section 8.2 discusses the evaluation results.

8.1 Levels of Protection

In order to display the evaluation results in a meaningful format, the percutaneous protective garments were grouped into the EPA levels of protection as well as on configuration of the garments. The garments in this section are identified as EPA Level A encapsulated suits and ensembles, EPA Level B encapsulated suits, coveralls, garments, and ensembles with level of protection not provided.

- **EPA Level A** garments are gas-tight. They provide a protective barrier that completely covers the wearer and their respirators.

- **EPA Level B** garments are liquid splash-protective. They are available as nongas-tight encapsulating suits, coveralls, or two-piece overgarments. The material is impermeable and offers splash protection but not continuous liquid contact or vapor protection. For those preferring additional protection for their respiratory equipment, EPA Level B encapsulated suits are available. These suits cannot be substituted for EPA Level A suits however, because the seams and zippers are not gas tight.

- There are other protective suits and garments, made of traditional textiles that allow vapors and liquids to pass through. They do not offer protection against highly toxic CB and TIMs. This category includes several EPA Level C garments and other garments that have no protective level designation.

8.2 Evaluation Results

The evaluation results for the percutaneous protective garments are presented in tabular format for the 180 pieces of equipment identified at the time this guide was written. A table is presented for each of the identified categories. Each table includes the specific equipment and the symbol that corresponds to how the equipment item was characterized based upon each of the selection factor definitions. The acronym "TBD" is displayed in the appropriate cell if data were not available to characterize a specific selection factor. The acronym "NA" is displayed in the appropriate cell if the data were not applicable for a piece of equipment. The results of categorizing the percutaneous protective garments are presented in table 8–1.

Table 8–1. Percutaneous protective garments

	Percutaneous Protective Garments				
	Encapsulating	Ensembles	Coveralls	Overgarments	Total
EPA Level A	43	4			47
EPA Level B	29		89		118
Other		6		9	15
Total	**72**	**10**	**89**	**9**	**180**

Table 8–2 provides the table number and associated table pages for each of the usage categories.

Table 8–2. Evaluation results reference table

Table Name	Table Number	Page(s)
Percutaneous protection (EPA Level A encapsulating)	8–3	61–65
Percutaneous protection (EPA Level A ensembles)	8–4	66
Percutaneous protection (EPA Level B encapsulating)	8–5	67–70
Percutaneous protection (coveralls)	8–6	71–79
Percutaneous protection (ensembles)	8–7	80
Percutaneous protection (overgarments)	8–8	81
Selection factor key for percutaneous protection (garments)	8–9	82

Table 8–3 and table 8–4 detail the evaluation results for the EPA Level A encapsulated and ensembles.

Tables 8–5 and 8–6 detail the evaluation results for EPA Level B encapsulating and coveralls.

Tables 8–7 and 8–8 detail the evaluation for other percutaneous protection ensembles and overgarments.

Table 8-3. Percutaneous protection (EPA Level A encapsulating)

August 2001

ID #	Name	Certifications/Regulations*
1	STEPO Chemical Protective Suit (Totally encapsulating)	Type Classified by U.S. Army, 1997
2	Tychem® 10000 Commander Level A Fully Encapsulating Suit	NA
3	Tychem® 10000 Commander Level A Fully Encapsulating Suit	NA
4	Tychem® 10000 Commander Level A Fully Encapsulating Suit	NA
5	Tychem® 10000 Commander Level A Fully Encapsulating Suit	NA
6	Tychem® 10000 EX Commander Level A Fully Encapsulating Suit	NA
7	Tychem® 10000 EX Commander Level A Fully Encapsulating Suit	NA
8	Tychem® 10000 EX Commander Level A Fully Encapsulating Suit	NA
9	Tychem® 10000 EX Commander Level A Fully Encapsulating Suit	NA

Selection factor columns (rated with graphical fill symbols): Chemical Agents Protection, Biological Agents Protection, TIMs Protection, Duration of Protection, Environmental Conditions, Weight/Comfort, Dexterity/Mobility (Ease of Use), Sizes Available, Visibility, Launderability, Training Requirements, Unit Cost.

'NA' - the specific selection factor is not applicable for the piece of equipment.
'TBD' (to be determined) - there is currently no data available to support that selection factor.
See Table 8-9 for selection factor definitions.
* See Appendix B, References, number eight.

Table 8-3. Percutaneous protection (EPA Level A encapsulating)-Continued
August 2001

ID #	Name	Certifications/Regulations*	Chemical Agents Protection	Biological Agents Protection	TIMs Protection	Duration of Protection	Environmental Conditions	Weight/Comfort	Dexterity/Mobility (Ease of use)	Sizes Available	Visibility	Launderability	Training Requirements	Unit Cost
62	Kappler Responder® CSM OSHA Level A	Each Government has developed its own internal guidance for storage and use	●	TBD	TBD	TBD	●	●	●	TBD	○	○	●	●
66	Lakeland Tychem® 10000 Economy Level A Encapsulated Suit	OSHA Level A, ASTM F1052	●	◐	●	●	●	●	●	●	◔	◐	◐	TBD
67	Lakeland Tychem® 10000 Economy Level A Encapsulated Suit	OSHA Level A, ASTM F1052	●	◐	●	●	●	●	●	●	◔	◐	◐	TBD
68	Lakeland Tychem® 10000 Level A Suit	OSHA Level A, ASTM F1052	●	◐	●	●	●	●	●	●	◔	●	●	TBD
79	Trelchem® High Performance Suit (HPS) Level A	NFPA 1991/2000 (USA), EN9 (European); ASTM F739	◐	◐	●	●	◐	●	●	●	●	◐	◐	●
80	Trelchem® TLU (Limited Use) Level A	NFPA 1991/2000 (USA), EN943 (European)	TBD	◐	●	●	◐	●	●	◔	○	◐	◐	◐
81	Trelchem® Vapor Barrier Suit (VPI) Level A	NFPA 1991/2000 (USA), EN943 (European), ASTM F739	TBD	◐	●	●	◐	●	●	◔	●	◐	●	●
82	Trelchem® Vapor Barrier Suit (VPS) Level A	NFPA 1991/2000 (USA), EN943 (European), ASTM F739	TBD	◐	●	●	◐	●	●	◔	●	◐	◐	●

'NA' - the specific selection factor is not applicable for the piece of equipment.
'TBD' (to be determined) - there is currently no data available to support that selection factor.
See Table 8-9 for selection factor definitions.
* See Appendix B, References, number eight.

62

Table 8-3. Percutaneous protection (EPA Level A encapsulating)-Continued

August 2001

Legend for rating symbols: ● = full, ◐ = half, ◔ = quarter, ○ = empty.

ID #	Name	Certifications/Regulations*	Chemical Agents Protection	Biological Agents Protection	TIMs Protection	Duration of Protection	Environmental Conditions	Weight/Comfort	Dexterity/Mobility (Ease of Use)	Sizes Available	Visibility	Launderability	Training Requirements	Unit Cost
47	Chemturion® Suit: Model 35 Level A Laboratory Suit, Reusable	Not applicable for reusable Level A suits	◐	TBD	TBD	●	●	●	◐	●	●	●	TBD	TBD
48	Chemturion® Suit: Ready 1 Model 91 Level A Limited Use Chemical Protective Suit	None	●	●	●	●	●	●	◐	●	◔	●	◐	◐
49	Chemturion® Suit: Model 84 Level A Total Encapsulating Suit, Reusable	Not applicable for reusable Level A suits	◐	TBD	TBD	●	●	●	◐	●	●	●	TBD	TBD
50	Kappler Responder® Total Encapsulating Level A (Gas-tight) Suit	OSHA 1910.132 and OSHA 1910.120	●	TBD	TBD	●	●	TBD	●	TBD	○	◐	TBD	TBD
51	Kappler Responder® Total Encapsulating Level A Suit	OSHA 1910.132 and OSHA 1910.120	●	TBD	TBD	●	●	TBD	●	TBD	○	◐	TBD	TBD
52	Kappler Total Encapsulating Level A Suit	OSHA 1910.132 and OSHA 1910.120	NA	TBD	●	●	●	TBD	●	TBD	○	◐	TBD	TBD
53	Kappler Responder® Plus Total Encapsulating Level A Suit	OSHA 1910.132 and OSHA 1910.120	NA	◐	●	●	●	◐	●	TBD	○	◐	TBD	TBD
54	Kappler Responder® Total Encapsulating Level A Suit, NFPA 1991 (Vapor Protective)	NFPA 1991, 2000 Edition (to comply with NFPA 1991 certification, must be worn with aluminized overcover), OSHA 1910.132, OSHA 1910.120	NA	TBD	TBD	●	●	TBD	●	TBD	○	◐	●	●

'NA' - the specific selection factor is not applicable for the piece of equipment.

'TBD' (to be determined) - there is currently no data available to support that selection factor.

See Table 8-9 for selection factor definitions.

* See Appendix B, References, number eight.

63

Table 8-3. Percutaneous protection (EPA Level A encapsulating)-Continued
August 2001

ID #	Name	Certifications/Regulations*	Chemical Agents Protection	Biological Agents Protection	Tims Protection	Duration of Protection	Environmental Conditions	Weight/Comfort	Dexterity/Mobility (Ease of Use)	Sizes Available	Visibility	Launderability	Training Requirements	Unit Cost
19	Tychem® TK Commander Level A Fully Encapsulating Suit	Will meet the requirements of NFPA 1992 - 2000 edition												
20	Tychem® TK Commander Level A Fully Encapsulating Suit	Will meet the requirements of NFPA 1992 - 2000 edition												
21	Tychem® TK Commander Level A Fully Encapsulating Suit	Will meet the requirements of NFPA 1992 - 2000 edition												
23	Tychem® TK EX Commander Level A Fully Encapsulating Suit	Will meet the requirements of NFPA 1992 - 2000 edition												
24	Tychem® TK EX Commander Level A Fully Encapsulating Suit	Will meet the requirements of NFPA 1992 - 2000 edition												
25	Tychem® TK EX Commander Level A Fully Encapsulating Suit	Will meet the requirements of NFPA 1992 - 2000 edition												
26	Tychem® TK EX Commander Level A Fully Encapsulating Suit	Will meet the requirements of NFPA 1992 - 2000 edition												
43	Disposable Toxicological Agent Protective Suit (DTAP)/Level A	ASTM F 1359-97; NFPA 1991, ASTM D3786, ASTM D5034, ASTM D1117; will be NFPA 1994 certified		TBD	TBD									
46	Chemturion® Suit: Model 13 Level A (SCBA), Reusable	Not applicable for reusable Level A suits												

'NA' - the specific selection factor is not applicable for the piece of equipment.
'TBD' (to be determined) - there is currently no data available to support that selection factor.
See Table 8-9 for selection factor definitions.
* See Appendix B, References, number eight.

Table 8-3. Percutaneous protection (EPA Level A encapsulating)–Continued
August 2001

ID #	Name	Certifications/Regulations*	Chemical Agents Protection	Biological Agents Protection	TIMs Protection	Duration of Protection	Environmental Conditions	Weight/Comfort	Dexterity/Mobility (Ease of Use)	Sizes Available	Visibility	Launderability	Training Requirements	Unit Cost
10	Tychem® BR Commander Level A Fully Encapsulating Suit	Will meet the requirements of NFPA 1992 - 2000 edition	●	●	◐	●	●	◐	●	◕	◔	●	◐	
11	Tychem® BR Commander Level A Fully Encapsulating Suit	Will meet the requirements of NFPA 1992 - 2000 edition	●	●	◐	●	●	◐	●	●	◔	●	◐	
12	Tychem® BR Commander Level A Fully Encapsulating Suit	Will meet the requirements of NFPA 1992 - 2000 edition	●	●	◐	●	●	◐	●	●	◔	●	◐	
13	Tychem® BR Commander Level A Fully Encapsulating Suit	Will meet the requirements of NFPA 1992 - 2000 edition	●	●	◐	●	●	◐	●	●	◔	●	◐	
14	Tychem® BR EX Commander Level A Fully Encapsulating Suit	Will meet the requirements of NFPA 1992 - 2000 edition	●	●	◐	●	●	◐	●	●	◔	●	◐	
15	Tychem® BR EX Commander Level A Fully Encapsulating Suit	Will meet the requirements of NFPA 1992 - 2000 edition	●	●	◐	●	●	◐	●	●	◔	●	◐	
16	Tychem® BR EX Commander Level A Fully Encapsulating Suit	Will meet the requirements of NFPA 1992 - 2000 edition	●	●	◐	●	●	◐	●	●	◔	●	◐	
17	Tychem® BR EX Commander Level A Fully Encapsulating Suit	Will meet the requirements of NFPA 1992 - 2000 edition	●	●	◐	●	●	◐	●	●	◔	●	◐	
18	Tychem® TK Commander Level A Fully Encapsulating Suit	Will meet the requirements of NFPA 1992 - 2000 edition	●	●	◐	●	●	◐	●	●	◔	●	◐	

'NA' - the specific selection factor is not applicable for the piece of equipment.
'TBD' (to be determined) - there is currently no data available to support that selection factor.
See Table 8-9 for selection factor definitions.
* See Appendix B, References, number eight.

Table 8-4. Percutaneous protection (EPA Level A ensembles)
August 2001

ID #	Name	Certifications/Regulations*	Chemical Agents Protection	Biological Agents Protection	TIMs Protection	Duration of Protection	Environmental Conditions	Weight/Comfort	Dexterity/Mobility (Ease of Use)	Sizes Available	Visibility	Launderability	Training Requirements	Unit Cost
22	Tychem® TK EX Commander Brigade Level A Ensemble	NFPA 1991-2000 certified	●	◐	●	●	◐	●	●	●	◔	●	●	●
64	Lakeland Tychem® 10000 NFPA Certified Level A Ensemble	NFPA 1991-2000 edition, ASTM F1052	●	◐	●	●	○	●	●	●	◔	◐	◐	TBD
65	Lakeland Tychem® 10000 Level A Ensemble	NFPA 1991-2000 edition, ASTM F1052	●	◐	●	●	○	TBD	●	●	◔	◐	◐	TBD
145	Kappler Ensemble, EPA Level A	NFPA 1991, 2000	●	TBD	NA	○	●	TBD	●	◐	◔	◐	○	○

'NA' - the specific selection factor is not applicable for the piece of equipment.
'TBD' (to be determined) - there is currently no data available to support that selection factor.
See Table 8-9 for selection factor definitions.
* See Appendix B, References, number eight.

66

Table 8-5. Percutaneous protection (EPA Level B encapsulating)
August 2001

ID #	Name	Certifications/Regulations*	Chemical Agents Protection	Biological Agents Protection	TIMs Protection	Duration of Protection	Environmental Conditions	Weight/Comfort	Dexterity/Mobility (Ease of Use)	Sizes Available	Visibility	Launderability	Training Requirements	Unit Cost
27	Tychem® 10000 Level B Fully Encapsulating Suit	NA												
28	Tychem® 10000 Level B Fully Encapsulating Suit	NA												
29	Tychem® 10000 Deluxe Level B Fully Encapsulating Suit	NA												
30	Tyvek® Level B Fully Encapsulating Suit	NA	NA	TBD	TBD	TBD								
31	Tychem® QC Level B Fully Encapsulating Suit	NA	TBD		TBD									
32	Tychem® SL Utility Level B Encapsulating Suit	NA												
33	Tychem® SL Utility Level B Encapsulating Suit	NA												
34	Tychem® SL Level B Fully Encapsulating Suit	NA												
35	Tychem® SL Level B Fully Encapsulating Suit	NA												
36	Tychem® QC Level B Fully Encapsulating Suit	NA	TBD											

'NA' - the specific selection factor is not applicable for the piece of equipment.
'TBD' (to be determined) - there is currently no data available to support that selection factor.
See Table 8-9 for selection factor definitions.
* See Appendix B, References, number eight.

Table 8-5. Percutaneous protection (EPA Level B encapsulating)—Continued
August 2001

ID #	Name	Certifications/ Regulations*	Chemical Agents Protection	Biological Agents Protection	TIMs Protection	Duration of Protection	Environmental Conditions	Weight/Comfort	Dexterity/Mobility (Ease of Use)	Sizes Available	Visibility	Launderability	Training Requirements	Unit Cost
37	Tychem® BR Level B Fully Encapsulating Suit	NA												
38	Tychem® BR Level B Fully Encapsulating Suit	NA												
39	Tychem® BR Deluxe Level B Fully Encapsulating Suit	NA												
40	Tychem® TK Level B Fully Encapsulating Suit	NA												
41	Tychem® TK Level B Fully Encapsulating Suit	NA												
42	Tychem® TK Deluxe Level B Fully Encapsulating Suit	NA												
44	Disposable Toxicological Agent Protective Suit (DTAP)/Level B	ASTM F 1359-97; NFPA 1991, ASTM D3786, ASTM D5034, ASTM D1117; will be NFPA 1994 certified												
56	Kappler Total Encapsulating Level B Suit	OSHA 1910.132 and OSHA 1910.120	NA	TBD	TBD					TBD			TBD	
57	Kappler CPF 3 Total Encapsulating Level B Suit	OSHA 1910.132 and OSHA 1910.120	NA	TBD	TBD					TBD				

'NA' - the specific selection factor is not applicable for the piece of equipment.
'TBD' (to be determined) - there is currently no data available to support that selection factor.
See Table 8-9 for selection factor definitions.
* - See Appendix B, References, number eight.

Table 8-5. Percutaneous protection (EPA Level B encapsulating)-Continued
August 2001

ID #	Name	Certifications/Regulations	Chemical Agents Protection*	Biological Agents Protection	TIMs Protection	Duration of Protection	Environmental Conditions	Weight/Comfort	Dexterity/Mobility (Ease of Use)	Sizes Available	Visibility	Launderability	Training Requirements	Unit Cost
58	Kappler Responder® Total Encapsulating Level B (Liquid Protective) Suit	OSHA 1910.132 and 1910.120	●	NA	TBD	TBD	●	TBD	◕	●	TBD	○	◐	TBD
59	Kappler CPF 4 Total Encapsulating Level B Suit	OSHA 1910.120	○	NA	◐	●	●	●	◔	●	TBD	○	◐	TBD
60	Kappler CPF 4 Total Encapsulating Level B Suit	OSHA 1910.120	○	NA	◐	●	●	●	◕	●	TBD	○	◐	TBD
61	Kappler Responder® Total Encapsulating Level B Suit (liquid protective)	None	●	NA	TBD	TBD	●	●	◕	●	TBD	○	◐	TBD
63	Kappler Responder® CS OSHA Level B	Each Government has developed its own internal guidance for storage and use	●	TBD	TBD	TBD	●	●	●	●	TBD	○	○	●
69	Lakeland Tychem® 9400 Level B Encapsulated Suit	NA	●	TBD	◐	●	◐	●	●	●	●	◔	●	TBD
70	Lakeland Tychem® 9400 Level B Encapsulated Suit	NA	●	TBD	◐	●	◐	●	●	●	●	◔	●	TBD
71	Lakeland Tychem® SL Level B Encapsulated Suit	NA	◐	TBD	◐	●	◐	●	●	●	●	◔	●	TBD
72	Lakeland Tychem® 10000 Level B Encapsulated Suit	NA	●	●	◐	●	●	●	●	●	●	◔	●	TBD

'NA' - the specific selection factor is not applicable for the piece of equipment.
'TBD' (to be determined) - there is currently no data available to support that selection factor.
See Table 8-9 for selection factor definitions.
* See Appendix B, References, number eight.

Table 8-5. Percutaneous protection (EPA Level B encapsulating)-Continued
August 2001

ID #	Name	Certifications/Regulations*	Chemical Agents Protection	Biological Agents Protection	TIMs Protection	Duration of Protection	Environmental Conditions	Weight/Comfort	Dexterity/Mobility (Ease of Use)	Sizes Available	Visibility	Launderability	Training Requirements	Unit Cost
73	Lakeland Tychem® 10000 Level B Coverall	NA	●	●	◐	●	●	●	●	●	●	◔	●	TBD

'NA' - the specific selection factor is not applicable for the piece of equipment.
'TBD' (to be determined) - there is currently no data available to support that selection factor.
See Table 8-9 for selection factor definitions.
* See Appendix B, References, number eight.

Table 8-6. Percutaneous protection (coveralls)
August 2001

#	Name	Certifications/Regulations*	Chemical Agents Protection	Biological Agents Protection	TIMs Protection	Duration of Protection	Environmental Conditions	Weight/Comfort	Dexterity/Mobility (Ease of Use)	Sizes Available	Visibility	Launderability	Training Requirements	Unit Cost
87	CCA_DuPont Tyvek® F Coverall	CE Certification	◐	◐	◐	◐	TBD	●	●	●	NA	NA	●	●
88	Tychem® 10000 Coverall	NA	●	◐	◐	●	●	●	●	●	NA	◔	●	●
89	Tychem® 10000 Coverall	NA	●	◐	◐	●	●	●	●	●	NA	◔	●	●
90	Tychem® 10000 Coverall	NA	●	◐	◐	●	●	●	●	●	NA	◔	●	◐
91	Tychem® 10000 Coverall	NA	●	◐	◐	●	●	●	●	●	NA	◔	●	●
92	Tychem® 10000 Coverall	NA	●	◐	◐	●	●	●	●	●	NA	◔	●	●
93	Tychem® 10000 Coverall	NA	●	◐	◐	●	●	●	●	●	NA	◔	●	◐
94	Tychem® 10000 Coverall	NA	●	◐	◐	●	●	●	●	●	NA	◔	●	◐
95	Tyvek® Coverall	NA	NA	◐	TBD	TBD	●	●	●	●	NA	◔	●	●
96	Tyvek® Coverall	NA	NA	◐	TBD	TBD	●	●	●	●	NA	◔	●	●
97	Tyvek® Coverall	NA	NA	◐	TBD	TBD	●	●	●	●	NA	◔	●	●
98	Tyvek® Coverall	NA	NA	◐	TBD	TBD	●	●	●	●	NA	◔	●	●

'NA' - the specific selection factor is not applicable for the piece of equipment.
'TBD' (to be determined) - there is currently no data available to support that selection factor.
See Table 8-9 for selection factor definitions.
* See Appendix B, References, number eight.

Table 8-6. Percutaneous protection (coveralls)-Continued
August 2001

ID #	Name	Certifications/ Regulations*	Chemical Agents Protection	Biological Agents Protection	TIMs Protection	Duration of Protection	Environmental Conditions	Weight/ Comfort	Dexterity/ Mobility (Ease of Use)	Sizes Available	Visibility	Launderability	Training Requirements	Unit Cost
99	Tyvek® Coverall	NA	NA	TBD	TBD	TBD	●	●	●	●	NA	◔	●	●
100	Tychem® QC Coverall	NA	TBD	◐	◐	◐	●	●	●	●	NA	◔	●	●
101	Tychem® QC Coverall	NA	TBD	◐	◐	◐	●	●	●	●	NA	◔	●	●
102	Tychem® QC Coverall	NA	TBD	◐	◐	◐	●	●	●	●	NA	◔	●	●
103	Tychem® QC Coverall	NA	TBD	◐	◐	◐	●	●	●	●	NA	◔	●	●
104	Tychem® QC Coverall	NA	TBD	◐	◐	◐	●	●	●	●	NA	◔	●	●
105	Tychem® QC Coverall	NA	TBD	◐	◐	◐	●	●	●	●	NA	◔	●	●
106	Tychem® QC Coverall	NA	TBD	◐	◐	◐	●	●	●	●	NA	◔	●	●
107	Tychem® QC Coverall	NA	TBD	◐	◐	◐	●	●	●	●	NA	◔	●	●
108	Tychem® QC Coverall	NA	TBD	◐	◐	◐	●	●	●	●	NA	◔	●	●

'NA' - the specific selection factor is not applicable for the piece of equipment.
'TBD' (to be determined) - there is currently no data available to support that selection factor.
See Table 8-9 for selection factor definitions.
* See Appendix B, References, number eight.

Table 8-6. Percutaneous protection (coveralls)–Continued
August 2001

ID #	Name	Certifications/Regulations*	Chemical Agents Protection	Biological Agents Protection	TIMs Protection	Duration of Protection	Environmental Conditions	Weight/Comfort	Dexterity/Mobility (Ease of Use)	Sizes Available	Visibility	Launderability	Training Requirements	Unit Cost
109	Tychem® QC Coverall	NA	TBD	◐	◐	◑	●	●	●	NA	◔	●	●	●
110	Tychem® SL Coverall	NA	◐	◐	◐	●	●	●	●	NA	◔	●	●	●
111	Tychem® SL Coverall	NA	◐	◐	◐	●	●	●	●	NA	◔	●	●	●
112	Tychem® SL Coverall	NA	◐	◐	◐	●	●	●	●	NA	◔	●	●	●
113	Tychem® SL Coverall	NA	◐	◐	◐	●	●	●	●	NA	◔	●	●	●
114	Tychem® SL Coverall	NA	◐	◐	◐	●	●	●	●	NA	◔	●	●	●
115	Tychem® SL Coverall	NA	◐	◐	◐	●	●	●	●	NA	◔	●	●	●
116	Tychem® SL Coverall	NA	◐	◐	◐	●	●	●	●	NA	◔	●	●	●
117	Tychem® SL Coverall	NA	◐	◐	◐	●	●	●	●	NA	◔	●	●	●
118	Tychem® SL Coverall	NA	◐	◐	◐	●	●	●	●	NA	◔	●	●	●

'NA' - the specific selection factor is not applicable for the piece of equipment.
'TBD' (to be determined) - there is currently no data available to support that selection factor.
See Table 8-9 for selection factor definitions.
* See Appendix B, References, number eight.

73

Table 8-6. Percutaneous protection (coveralls)-Continued
August 2001

ID #	Name	Certifications/ Regulations*	Chemical Agents Protection	Biological Agents Protection	TIMs Protection	Duration of Protection	Environmental Conditions	Weight/ Comfort	Dexterity/ Mobility (ease of Use)	Sizes Available	Visibility	Launderability	Training Requirements	Unit Cost
119	Tychem® SL Coverall	NA	◐	◐	●	●	●	●	●	●	NA	◔	●	●
120	Tychem® QC Coverall	NA	TBD	◐	TBD	●	●	●	●	●	NA	◔	●	●
121	Tychem® QC Coverall	NA	TBD	◐	TBD	●	●	●	●	●	NA	◔	●	●
122	Tychem® QC Coverall	NA	TBD	◐	TBD	●	●	●	●	●	NA	◔	●	●
123	Tychem® QC Coverall	NA	TBD	◐	TBD	●	●	●	●	●	NA	◔	●	●
124	Tychem® QC Coverall	NA	TBD	◐	TBD	●	●	●	●	●	NA	◔	●	●
125	Tychem® BR Coverall	NA	●	◐	●	●	●	●	●	●	NA	◔	●	●
126	Tychem® BR Coverall	NA	●	◐	●	●	●	●	●	●	NA	◔	●	●
127	Tychem® BR Coverall	NA	●	◐	●	●	●	●	●	●	NA	◔	●	●
128	Tychem® BR Coverall	NA	●	◐	●	●	●	●	●	●	NA	◔	●	●

'NA' - the specific selection factor is not applicable for the piece of equipment.
'TBD' (to be determined) - there is currently no data available to support that selection factor.
See Table 8-9 for selection factor definitions.
* See Appendix B, References, number eight.

74

Table 8-6. Percutaneous protection (coveralls)-Continued
August 2001

ID #	Name	Certifications/Regulations*	Chemical Agents Protection	Biological Agents Protection	TIMs Protection	Duration of Protection	Environmental Conditions	Weight/Comfort	Dexterity/Mobility (Ease of Use)	Sizes Available	Visibility	Launderability	Training Requirements	Unit Cost
129	Tychem® BR Coverall	NA								NA				
130	Tychem® BR Coverall	NA								NA				
131	Tychem® BR Coverall	NA								NA				
132	Tychem® TK Coverall	NA								NA				
133	Tychem® TK Coverall	NA								NA				
134	Tychem® TK Coverall	NA								NA				
135	Tychem® TK Coverall	NA								NA				
136	Tychem® TK Coverall	NA								NA				
137	Tychem® TK Coverall	NA								NA				
138	Tychem® TK Coverall	NA								NA				

NA' - the specific selection factor is not applicable for the piece of equipment.
'TBD' (to be determined) - there is currently no data available to support that selection factor.
See Table 8-9 for selection factor definitions.
* See Appendix B, References, number eight.

75

Table 8-6. Percutaneous protection (coveralls)-Continued
August 2001

ID #	Name	Certifications/Regulations	Chemical Agents Protection*	Biological Agents Protection	TIMS Protection	Duration of Protection	Environmental Conditions	Weight/Comfort	Dexterity/Mobility (Ease of Use)	Sizes Available	Visibility	Launderability	Training Requirements	Unit Cost
139	Kappler Coverall	OSHA 1910.132 and OSHA 1910.120	◐	NA	TBD	TBD	●	●	TBD	●	NA	TBD	●	TBD
140	Kappler Coverall	OSHA 1910.132 and OSHA 1910.120	◐	NA	TBD	TBD	●	●	TBD	●	NA	TBD	●	TBD
141	Kappler CPF 3 Coverall	OSHA 1910.132 and OSHA 1910.120	◐	NA	TBD	TBD	●	●	TBD	●	NA	TBD	●	◐
142	Kappler Responder® Level B Coverall	OSHA 1910.132 and OSHA 1910.120	●	NA	TBD	TBD	●	●	TBD	●	NA	TBD	●	TBD
143	Kappler Responder® Level B Coverall	OSHA 1910.132 and OSHA 1910.120	●	NA	TBD	TBD	●	●	TBD	●	NA	TBD	●	TBD
144	Kappler Responder® Level B Coverall	OSHA 1910.132 and OSHA 1910.120	●	NA	TBD	TBD	●	●	TBD	●	NA	TBD	●	TBD
146	Kappler CPF 4 Coverall	OSHA 1910.132 and OSHA 1910.120	○	NA	◐	●	●	●	TBD	●	NA	TBD	●	TBD
147	Kappler CPF 3 Coverall	OSHA 1910.132 and OSHA 1910.120	◐	NA	TBD	TBD	●	●	TBD	●	NA	TBD	●	TBD
148	Kappler CPF 4 Coverall	OSHA 1910.132 and OSHA 1910.120	○	NA	◐	●	●	●	TBD	●	NA	TBD	●	TBD
149	Kappler CPF 3 Coverall	NA	◐	NA	TBD	TBD	●	●	TBD	●	NA	TBD	●	TBD

'NA' - the specific selection factor is not applicable for the piece of equipment.
'TBD' (to be determined) - there is currently no data available to support that selection factor.
See Table 8-9 for selection factor definitions.
* See Appendix B, References, number eight.

Table 8-6. Percutaneous protection (coveralls)-Continued
August 2001

ID #	Name	Certifications/Regulations*	Chemical Agents Protection	Biological Agents Protection	TIMs Protection	Duration of Protection	Environmental Conditions	Weight/Comfort	Dexterity/Mobility (Ease of Use)	Sizes Available	Visibility	Launderability	Training Requirements	Unit Cost
164	Lakeland Tychem® SL Level B Coverall	NA	◑	TBD	◑	◑	●	●	●	◕	◔	●	TBD	
174	Lakeland Tychem® 9400 Level B Coverall	NA	●	TBD	◑	◑	●	●	●	◕	◔	●	TBD	
167	Lakeland Tychem® SL Level B Coverall	NA	◑	TBD	◑	◑	●	●	●	◕	◔	●	TBD	
162	Lakeland Tyvek® QC Level B Coverall	NA	○		◑	◑	●	●	●	◕	◔	●	TBD	
161	Lakeland Tyvek® QC Level B Coverall	NA	○		◑	◑	●	●	●	◕	◔	●	TBD	
163	Lakeland Tyvek® QC Level B Coverall	NA	○		◑	◑	●	●	●	◕	◔	●	TBD	
160	Lakeland Tyvek® QC Level B Coverall	NA	○		◑	◑	●	●	●	◕	◔	●	TBD	
172	Lakeland Tychem® 9400 Level B Coverall	NA	●	TBD	◑	◑	●	●	●	◕	◔	●	TBD	
158	Lakeland Tyvek® QC Level B Coverall	NA	○	TBD	◑	◑	●	●	●	◕	◔	●	TBD	
170	Lakeland Tychem® 9400 Level B Coverall	NA	●	TBD	◑	◑	●	●	●	◕	◔	●	TBD	

'NA' - the specific selection factor is not applicable for the piece of equipment.
'TBD' (to be determined) - there is currently no data available to support that selection factor.
See Table 8-9 for selection factor definitions.
* See Appendix B, References, number eight.

Table 8-6. Percutaneous protection (coveralls)-Continued
August 2001

ID #	Name	Certifications/Regulations*	Chemical Agents Protection	Biological Agents Protection	TIMs Protection	Duration of Protection	Environmental Conditions	Weight/Comfort	Dexterity/Mobility (Ease of Use)	Sizes Available	Visibility	Launderability	Training Requirements	Unit Cost
165	Lakeland Tychem® SL Level B Coverall	NA	◐	TBD	◐	●	◐	●	●	●	◔	●	◔	TBD
166	Lakeland Tychem® SL Level B Coverall	NA	◐	TBD	◐	●	◐	●	●	●	◔	●	◔	TBD
157	Lakeland Tychem® 10000 Level B Coverall	NA	◐	TBD	◐	●	◐	●	●	●	◔	●	◔	TBD
153	Lakeland Tychem® 10000 Level B Coverall	NA	○	TBD	◐	●	◐	●	●	●	◔	●	◔	TBD
169	Lakeland Tychem® SL Level B Coverall	NA	◐	TBD	◐	●	●	●	●	●	◔	●	◔	TBD
159	Lakeland Tyvek QC Level B Coverall	NA	○	TBD	◐	●	●	●	●	●	◔	●	◔	TBD
168	Lakeland Tychem® SL Level B Coverall	NA	◐	TBD	◐	●	◐	●	●	●	◔	●	◔	TBD
171	Lakeland Tychem® 9400 Level B Coverall	NA	●	TBD	◐	●	◐	●	●	●	◔	●	◔	TBD
173	Lakeland Tychem® 9400 Level B Coverall	NA	●	TBD	◐	●	◐	●	●	●	◔	●	◔	TBD
150	Lakeland Tychem® 10000 Level B Coverall	NA	●	●	◐	●	●	●	●	●	◔	●	◔	TBD

'NA'- the specific selection factor is not applicable for the piece of equipment.
'TBD' (to be determined) - there is currently no data available to support that selection factor.
See Table 8-9 for selection factor definitions.
* See Appendix B, References, number eight.

Table 8-6. Percutaneous protection (coveralls)-Continued
August 2001

ID #	Name	Certifications/Regulations*	Chemical Agents Protection	Biological Agents Protection	TIMS Protection	Duration of Protection	Environmental Conditions	Weight/Comfort	Dexterity/Mobility (Ease of Use)	Sizes Available	Visibility	Launderability	Training Requirements	Unit Cost
151	Lakeland Tychem® 10000 Level B Coverall	NA	●	◐	●	●	●	●	●	◕	◔	●	●	TBD
154	Lakeland Tychem® 10000 Level B Coverall	NA	●	◐	●	●	●	●	●	◕	◔	●	●	TBD
155	Lakeland Tychem® 10000 Level B Coverall	NA	●	◐	●	●	●	●	●	●	◔	●	●	TBD
152	Lakeland Tychem® 10000 Level B Coverall	NA	●	◐	●	●	●	●	●	◕	◔	●	●	TBD
156	Lakeland Tychem® 10000 Level B Coverall	NA	●	◐	●	●	●	●	●	●	◔	●	●	TBD
176	The US Air Force Saratoga CWU-66/P Chemical Protective Flight Coverall	U.S. and NATO military chemical protection specifications	●	○	●	●	●	●	●	●	◐	●	●	TBD
178	SEA Tyvl® F Suit	European standards	●	◐	●	●	●	●	○	○	NA	●	●	●

NA' - the specific selection factor is not applicable for the piece of equipment.
'TBD' (to be determined) - there is currently no data available to support that selection factor.
See Table 8-9 for selection factor definitions.
* See Appendix B, References, number eight.

Table 8-7. Percutaneous protection (ensembles - other)
August 2001

ID #	Name	Certifications/Regulations*	Chemical Agents Protection	Biological Agents Protection	TIMs Protection	Duration of Protection	Environmental Conditions	Weight/Comfort	Dexterity/Mobility (Ease or Use)	Sizes Available	Visibility	Launderability	Training Requirements	Unit Cost
74	C-Cover S-89 One Piece NBC Protective Overgarment (disposable)	Meets NATO Military Standards for NBC Ensemble Swedish Defense Lab Certification	●	●	◐	●	○	TBD	TBD	○	●	○	TBD	●
76	C-Cover Dress S-97 NBC Protective Overgarment (disposable)	NATO Military Standards for NBC Ensemble Swedish Defense Lab Certification	●	●	◐	●	●	TBD	TBD	○	●	○	●	◐
83	Disposable Toxicological Agent Protective Suit (DTAPS)/Level C1 (for field use)	ASTM F 1359-97, NFPA 1991, ASTM D3786, ASTM D5034, ASTM D1117; will be NFPA 1994 certified	◕	●	◐	●	◐	●	●	●	●	○	◕	●
84	Disposable Toxicological Agent Protective Suit (DTAPS)/Level C2 (for hospital use)	ASTM F 1359-97, NFPA 1991, ASTM D3786, ASTM D5034, ASTM D1117; will be NFPA 1994 certified	●	●	◔	●	●	●	●	●	◕	◑	◕	◐
85	Demilitarization Protective Ensembles (DPEs)	Not specified	TBD	TBD	TBD	TBD	TBD	TBD	TBD	TBD	TBD	TBD	TBD	TBD
86	"Hot" Operation: Air-Fed Garments	Not specified	TBD	TBD	TBD	TBD	TBD	TBD	TBD	TBD	TBD	TBD	TBD	TBD

"NA" - the specific selection factor is not applicable for the piece of equipment.
"TBD" (to be determined) - there is currently no data available to support that selection factor.
See Table 8-9 for selection factor definitions.
* See Appendix B, References, number eight.

Table 8-8. Percutaneous protection (overgarments)
August 2001

ID #	Name	Certifications/Regulations*	Chemical Agents Protection	Biological Agents Protection	TIMs Protection	Duration of Protection	Environmental Conditions	Weight/Comfort	Dexterity/Mobility (Ease of Use)	Sizes Available	Visibility	Launderability	Training Requirements	Unit Cost
45	EUROLITE NBC-Protection Suit	Products tested by TNO, which certifies NATO standard for our products.	●	●	◐	●	●	TBD	◐	◐	●	●	●	●
50	IPE (Individual Protection Equipment)	Canadian Department of National Defence	◐	○	TBD	●	●	◐	●	TBD	◕	●	●	◐
75	C-Cover S-99N (transparent body cover)	Not specified	◐	◐	TBD	●	●	●	NA	●	○	●	TBD	TBD
77	Saratoga HAMMER Suit	MIL-C-29462	●	●	○	●	●	●	●	●	◐	●	●	◐
78	Saratoga Joint Service Lightweight Integrated Suit (JSLIST)	DoD, U.S. and NATO military chemical protection specifications.	●	●	○	●	●	●	●	●	◐	●	●	◐
175	Chemical Protective Overgarments (CPO) LANX Fabric Systems	Specification MIL-U-44435. Governed by International Traffic and Arms Regulations (ITAR).	●	●	TBD	●	●	●	●	●	◐	●	TBD	TBD
177	CB Incident Emergency Escape Kit	Not specified	◐	TBD	TBD	◐	TBD	●	TBD	NA	◕	TBD	TBD	TBD
179	NewPac Cami Cover Dress C/91	EU directives 89/686/EEC; Article 10, New Pac TS C/9107-2	◐	◐	●	●	●	●	○	◐	NA	●	◐	◐
180	NewPac First Responder PPE Kit	EU directives 89/686/EEC; Article 10, and pending NFPA 1994. For APR: 42 CFR 84, pending NFPA 1994.	◐	◐	TBD	◐	●	●	○	◐	NA	●	◐	◐

'NA - the specific selection factor is not applicable for the piece of equipment.
'TBD' (to be determined) - there is currently no data available to support that selection factor.
See Table 8-9 for selection factor definitions.
* See Appendix B, References, number eight.

Table 8-9. Selection factor key for percutaneous protection (garments)
August 2001

Symbol	Chemical Agents Protection	Biological Agents Protection	TIMs Protection	Protection Duration	Environmental Conditions	Weight/Comfort	Dexterity/Mobility (Ease of Use)	Sizes Available	Visibility	Launderability	Training Requirements	Cost (Gas Tight)	Cost (Not Gas Tight)	Cost (Coveralls)
● (full)	Protects against all nerve and blister agents	Protects against all biological agents	Protects against all TIMs listed	Protects up to 2 h	Protects in all environments	Easily manageable, able to be worn for long periods with no effects	Not limiting	At least 5 sizes available	90 % to 100 % visibility	Able to be cleaned and reused greater than 50 times	Little to no training required	Less than or equal to $500 per unit	Less than or equal to $100 per unit	Less than or equal to $75 for single unit or $150 for bulk packaging
◕ (three-quarter)									75 % to 90 % visibility	Able to be cleaned and reused 25 to 50 times				
◑ (half)	Protects against some of the nerve and blister agents	Protects against some biological agents	Protects against multiple TIMs	Protects 30 min to 90 min	Protects in normal environments	Manageable, but unable to wear for more than 1 h to 2 h at a time	Some loss of mobility, range of motion	At least 4 sizes available	50 % to 75 % visibility	Able to be cleaned and reused 5 to 50 times	Some training required, 4 h or more	Greater than $500 but less than $1000 per unit	Greater than $100 but less than $500 per unit	Greater than $75 (single unit) or $150 (bulk) but less than $300 for single item or bulk packaging
◔ (quarter)										Not intended for reuse, but can be hand cleaned to remove dirt and dust				
○ (empty)	Protects against none of the blister or nerve agents	Protects against no biological agents	Protects against none of the TIMs listed	Protects less than 30 min	Protects only in specific environments	Very heavy and cumbersome, unable to wear for prolonged periods	Very limiting	One size fits all	Less than 50 % visibility	Unable to be reused	Continuous training required with recertification every few months	Greater than or equal to $1000 per unit	Greater than or equal to $500 per unit	Greater than or equal to $300 for single unit or bulk packaging

The blank cells designate that the symbol is not applicable for the selection factor.

9. EVALUATION OF PERCUTANEOUS PROTECTION (APPAREL)

The market survey (refer to sec. 2.0 of Vol. IIc) conducted for CB agent and TIM personal protective equipment identified 74 additional protective items (protective apparel). The details of the market survey, including data on each item, are provided in Volume IIc of this guide. This section documents the results of evaluating each item versus the 12 selection factors provided in section 6 of this volume. Section 9.1 identifies the types of protective apparel and section 9.2 discusses the evaluation results.

9.1 Protective Apparel

Other protective apparel includes ancillary clothing items and accessories that complete or supplement a particular protective ensemble (e.g., hoods, aprons, sleeves, gloves, boots, and boot covers). These items are generally intended for use in situations where the physical contact with hazardous material is limited and the hazard is completely characterized.

In order to display the evaluation results in a meaningful format, the apparel was grouped into the categories based on the type of protection that was provided and not the level of protection.

- **Hoods** provide a protective barrier that completely covers the heads and shoulders of the wearer and their respirator.

- **Foot protection** includes safety boots, boot covers, shoe covers, and socks. Some of these items are constructed to provide protection from crushing and others provide only barrier protection.

- **Hand protection** includes gloves (inner and outer) and sleeves. Like foot protection, some items afford abrasive protection while others provide only barrier protection.

- **Aprons, labcoats, and ponchos** provide barrier protection. They are available in a variety of configurations.

- **Undergarments** provide an extra level of protection.

- **Casualty bags** provide barrier protection.

- **Personal cooling equipment** are not true personal protective items, but they do reduce heat stress when worn with PPE.

9.2 Evaluation Results

The evaluation results for the percutaneous protective garments are presented in tabular format for the 74 pieces of protective apparel identified at the time this guide was written. A table is presented for each of the identified categories. Each table includes the specific equipment and the symbol that corresponds to how the equipment item was characterized based upon each of the selection factor definitions. The acronym "TBD" is displayed in the appropriate cell if data were not available to characterize a specific selection factor. The acronym "NA" is displayed in the appropriate cell if the data were not applicable for a piece of equipment. The results of categorizing the percutaneous protective apparel are presented in table 9–1.

Table 9–1. Percutaneous protective apparel

	Percutaneous Protective Items
Hoods	16
Foot protection	13
Hand protection	14
Shirts, pants, jackets, and overalls	12
Aprons, labcoats, and ponchos	10
Undergarments	2
Casualty bags	3
Personal cooling	4
Total	**74**

Table 9-2 provides the table number and associated table pages for each of the usage categories.

Table 9-2. Evaluation results reference table

Table Name	Table Number	Page(s)
Percutaneous protection (hoods)	9–3	86–87
Percutaneous protection (foot protection)	9–4	88–89
Percutaneous protection (hand protection)	9–5	90–91
Percutaneous protection (shirts, pants, jackets, and overalls)	9–6	92–93
Percutaneous protection (aprons, labcoats, and ponchos)	9–7	94
Percutaneous protection (undergarments)	9–8	95
Percutaneous protection (casualty bags)	9–9	96
Percutaneous protection (personal cooling)	9–10	97
Selection factor key for percutaneous protection (apparel)	9–11	98

Table 9–3 details the evaluation results for percutaneous protection (hoods).

Table 9–4 details the evaluation results for percutaneous protection (foot protection).

Table 9–5 details the evaluation results for percutaneous protection (hand protection).

Table 9–6 details the evaluation results for percutaneous protection (shirts, pants, jackets, and overalls).

Table 9–7 details the evaluation results for percutaneous protection (aprons, labcoats, and ponchos).

Table 9–8 details the evaluation results for percutaneous protection (undergarments).

Table 9–9 details the evaluation results for percutaneous protection (casualty bags).

Table 9–10 details the evaluation results for percutaneous (personal cooling).

Table 9–11 details the evaluation results for percutaneous protective equipment (apparel).

Table 9-3. Percutaneous protection (hoods)
August 2001

ID #	Name	Certifications/Regulations*	Chemical Agents Protection	Biological Agents Protection	TIMs Protection	Duration of Protection	Environmental Conditions	Weight/Comfort	Dexterity/Mobility (Ease of Use)	Available Sizes	Visibility	Launderability	Training Requirements	Unit Cost
18	Tyvek® Hood	ASTM D3776-85, ASTM D1777-64, ASTM D1682 (MD/CD), ASTM D1682 (MD/CD), ASTM D226 (MD/CD)	NA	TBD	TBD	TBD	●	●	◐	◐	◐	○	●	●
19	Tyvek® Hood	ASTM D3776-85, ASTM D1777-64, ASTM D1682 (MD/CD), ASTM D1682 (MD/CD), ASTM D226 (MD/CD)	NA	TBD	TBD	TBD	●	●	◐	◐	◐	○	●	●
20	Tyvek® Hood	ASTM D3776-85, ASTM D1777-64, ASTM D1682 (MD/CD), ASTM D1682 (MD/CD), ASTM D2261 (MD/CD)	NA	TBD	TBD	TBD	●	●	◐	◐	◐	○	●	●
24	Tychem® QC Hood	ASTM D3776-85, ASTM D1777-64, ASTM D3786-87, ASTM D1682-64, ASTM D1117-8	TBD	TBD	TBD	TBD	●	●	◐	◐	◐	◔	●	●
25	Tychem® QC Hood	ASTM D3776-85, ASTM D1777-64, ASTM D3786-87, ASTM D1682-64, ASTM D1117-8	TBD	TBD	TBD	TBD	●	●	◐	◐	◐	◔	●	●
26	Tychem® SL Hood	ASTM D3776-85, ASTM D1777-64, ASTM D3786-87, ASTM D1682-64, ASTM D1117	◐	TBD	TBD	●	●	●	◐	◐	◐	◔	●	●
27	Tychem® BR Hood/vest	ASTM D3776-85, ASTM D1777-64, ASTM D3787-89, ASTM D5034, ASTM D5597	●	TBD	◐	●	●	●	◐	◐	◐	◔	●	◐
28	Tychem® TK Hood/vest	ASTM D3776, ASTM D177, ASTM D3787, ASTM D15034, ASTM D5733	●	TBD	◐	●	●	●	◐	◐	◐	◔	●	◐
38	Kappler CPF 4 Hood	OSHA 1910.132 and OSHA 1910.120, ASTM D751 Test Battery	○	NA	◐	●	●	●	○	◐	◐	TBD	●	TBD

'NA' - the specific selection factor is not applicable for the piece of equipment.
'TBD' (to be determined) - there is currently no data available to support that selection factor.
See Table 9-11 for selection factor definitions.
* See Appendix B, References, number eight.

Table 9-3. Percutaneous protection (hoods)-Continued
August 2001

ID #	Name	Certifications/Regulations	Chemical Agents Protection*	Biological Agents Protection	TIMs Protection	Duration of Protection	Environmental Conditions	Weight/Comfort	Dexterity/Mobility (Ease of Use)	Available Sizes	Visibility	Launderability	Training Requirements	Unit Cost
42	Lakeland Tychem 10,000 Level B Hood	Not specified	●	●	◐	◐	●	●	○	◕	○	TBD	TBD	TBD
46	Tyvek QC Level B Hood	Not specified	TBD	TBD	TBD	TBD	●	●	●	◐	○	●	●	TBD
48	Tychem SL Level B Hood	Not specified	◐	TBD	TBD	●	●	●	●	◐	○	TBD	TBD	TBD
49	Tychem SL Level B Hood	Not specified	◐	TBD	TBD	●	●	●	●	◐	○	TBD	TBD	TBD
54	Lakeland Tychem 9400 Level B Hood	Not specified	●	TBD	◐	●	●	●	●	◐	○	TBD	TBD	TBD
55	Lakeland Tychem 9400 Level B Hood	Not specified	●	TBD	◐	●	●	●	●	●	○	●	●	TBD
70	Chemical-Biological Eye/Respiratory Disposable (C-BERD) Hood/Mask	After testing at SBCCOM in April under Test Support Agreement (TSA) program, will be submitted to C-BERD for NIOSH certification	●	●	◐	●	●	●	○	●	◔	●	●	●

'NA' - the specific selection factor is not applicable for the piece of equipment.
'TBD' (to be determined) - there is currently no data available to support that selection factor.
See Table 9-11 for selection factor definitions.
* See Appendix B, References, number eight.

87

Table 9-4. Percutaneous protection (foot protection)
August 2001

ID #	Name	Certifications/Regulations*	Chemical Agents Protection	Biological Agents Protection	TIMs Protection	Duration of Protection	Environmental Conditions	Weight/Comfort	Dexterity/Mobility (Ease of Use)	Available Sizes	Visibility	Launderability	Training Requirements	Unit Cost
1	Toxicological Agent Protective (TAP) Boot	CW Test Reports available (to 8 h requirement)	●	●	NA	●	●	TBD	●	NA	NA	◔	NA	◐
2	NBC Multipurpose Safety Boot	EN 345-2: 1997; CW Test Report from FOA Sweden available	●	●	TBD	●	●	TBD	●	NA	NA	◔	NA	◐
3	ACTON Basic NBC Overboot	CW and Physical Property Test Reports can be made available	●	●	NA	●	●	TBD	●	NA	NA	◔	NA	●
4	ACTON Lightweight NBC Overboot	CW and Physical Property Test Report available	●	●	NA	●	●	TBD	●	NA	NA	◔	NA	◐
7	Beta HazMat Boots	NFPA 199, 2000 Edition, ANSI Std Z41-PR, Z41 P199 I/75 C75, CSA Std Z195 M92 Grade 1	◐	◐	◐	●	TBD	TBD	●	NA	NA	TBD	●	TBD
8	Beta Boot/Shoe Covers	NFPA 199, 2000 Edition	◐	◐	◐	●	●	TBD	●	NA	NA	TBD	●	TBD
11	Chemical Biological Protective Sock	Meets NATO Military Standard and Tested to ERDEC Mil-Std by Natick	●	●	NA	●	●	●	◐	NA	NA	◔	●	◐
51	Tychem SL Level B Boots	Not specified	◐	TBD	TBD	●	●	●	○	NA	NA	○	TBD	TBD

'NA' - the specific selection factor is not applicable for the piece of equipment.
'TBD' (to be determined) - there is currently no data available to support that selection factor.
See Table 9-11 for selection factor definitions.
* See Appendix B, References, number eight.

Table 9-4. Percutaneous protection (foot protection)-Continued
August 2001

ID #	Name	Certifications/Regulations*	Chemical Agents Protection	Biological Agents Protection	TIMS Protection	Duration of Protection	Environmental Conditions	Weight/Comfort	Dexterity/Mobility (Ease of Use)	Available Sizes	Visibility	Launderability	Training Requirements	Unit Cost
56	Lakeland Tychem 9-400 Level B Boot Covers	Not specified	●	TBD	◐	●	●	●	●	○	NA	○	●	TBD
63	Rocky Shoes and Boots with Crosstech	NFPA 1999, Protective Clothing for Emergency Medical Operations (1992 edition), ASTM F 1671, ASTM F 903 (C)	TBD	◐	◐	TBD	TBD	●	●	●	NA	●	NA	◐
64	Servus HZT Hazmat Knee Boot	NFPA 1991 Requirements	TBD	TBD	TBD	TBD	TBD	TBD	●	●	NA	TBD	●	TBD
66	Saratoga Chemical Protective Socks	System chemical tests meet requirements of PD 97-04; Independent test data/certificate of compliance is available	●	●	◐	●	●	●	◐	◐	NA	◐	●	◐
68	Tingley Hazproof Overboot	SEI (Safety Equipment Institute); Tested chemical and physically per NFPA/SEI available	●	●	◐	●	●	●	●	●	NA	◕	●	◐

NA - the specific selection factor is not applicable for the piece of equipment.
'TBD' (to be determined) - there is currently no data available to support that selection factor.
See Table 9-11 for selection factor definitions.
* See Appendix B, References, number eight.

Table 9-5. Percutaneous protection (hand protection)
August 2001

ID #	Name	Certifications/Regulations*	Chemical Agents Protection	Biological Agents Protection	TIMs Protection	Duration of Protection	Environmental Conditions	Weight/Comfort	Dexterity/Mobility (Ease of Use)	Available Sizes	Visibility	Launderability	Training Requirements	Unit Cost
5	CB Moulded Glove With Liner	CW Test Information will be available in 2nd half of 2000	●	●	●	●	●	TBD	●	NA	◔	NA	●	
6	Ansell-Edmont Sol-Vex Gloves	ASTM standards; FDA-accepted materials	●	TBD	TBD	TBD	●	TBD	●	NA	TBD	●	TBD	
9	BUTYL PLUS - NBC/Toxic Protective Glove	Meets OSHA PPE and NATO Military Standard NATO/UK Spec SC/4986B, MIL G-12223J & OSHA PPE Std	●	●	TBD	●	●	●	◐	NA	◔	●	◐	
10	MULTI- PLUS - HAZMAT/Toxic Protective Glove	Meets OSHA PPE	TBD	TBD	TBD	●	●	●	◐	NA	●	●	●	
29	Integrated Chemical Biological Protective Glove	NATO Military Standard; NATO Standard Test Requirement for CB Ensemble	●	NA		●	●	●	◐	NA	◔	●	◐	
30	NBC gloves	Ministry of Defense, Austria; Test data can be obtained on request.	●	◐	●	●	●	●	◐	NA	◐	●	●	
33	Surgical Fit Gloves (CP-14F, CP-14FR, CP-7F)	ISO-9001 Registered	TBD	TBD	TBD	TBD	●	TBD	◐	NA	TBD	●	TBD	
34	Butyl Gloves	ISO-9001 Registered; ASTM F739-95 by TRI/Environmental, Inc. Manufactured according to Mil-G-43976, Mil-G-12223, and ZZ-G-381	●	◐	TBD	TBD	●	TBD	●	NA	TBD	●	TBD	

'NA' - the specific selection factor is not applicable for the piece of equipment.
'TBD' (to be determined) - there is currently no data available to support that selection factor.
See Table 9-11 for selection factor definitions.
* See Appendix B, References, number eight.

90

Table 9-5. Percutaneous protection (hand protection)-Continued
August 2001

ID #	Name	Certifications/Regulations*	Chemical Agents Protection	Biological Agents Protection	TIMS Protection	Duration of Protection	Environmental Conditions	Weight/Comfort	Dexterity/Mobility (Ease of Use)	Available Sizes	Visibility	Launderability	Training Requirements	Unit Cost
35	Neoprene Gloves	ISO-9001 Registered; Manufactured according to ZZ-G-381, NFPA 1992, NFPA 1991	●	TBD	◐	TBD	TBD	TBD	◐	NA	TBD	●	TBD	TBD
47	Tyvek QC Level B Sleeves	Not specified	TBD	TBD	TBD	TBD	●	●	○	NA	○	●	TBD	TBD
52	Tychem SL Level B Sleeves	Not specified	◐	TBD	●	●	●	●	○	NA	○	●	TBD	TBD
57	Lakeland Tychem 9400 Level B Sleeves	Not specified	●	TBD	●	●	●	●	○	NA	○	●	TBD	TBD
62	North Silver Shield Gloves	Not specified	TBD	TBD	TBD	TBD	TBD	TBD	◐	NA	TBD	●	TBD	TBD
65	Saratoga Chemical Protective Gloves	Meets CW agent protection requirements of MIL-C-29462 date 15 April 1992; Independent test data/certificate of compliance available upon request	●	●	◐	●	●	●	◐	NA	TBD	●	●	◐

'NA' - the specific selection factor is not applicable for the piece of equipment.
'TBD' (to be determined) - there is currently no data available to support that selection factor.
See Table 9-11 for selection factor definitions.
* See Appendix B, References, number eight.

Table 9-6. Percutaneous protection (shirts, pants, jackets, and overalls)
August 2001

ID #	Name	Certifications/Regulations*	Chemical Agents Protection	Biological Agents Protection	TMs Protection	Duration of Protection	Environmental Conditions	Weight/Comfort	Dexterity/Mobility (Ease of use)	Available Sizes	Visibility	Launderability	Training Requirements	Unit Cost
14	Tyvek® Shirt	ASTM D3776-85, ASTM D1777-64, ASTM D1682, ASTM D2261	NA	TBD	TBD	TBD	●	●	●	NA	○	●	●	●
17	Tyvek® Pants	ASTM D3776-85, ASTM D1777-64, ASTM D1682, ASTM D2261	NA	TBD	TBD	TBD	●	●	●	NA	○	●	●	●
22	Tychem® QC Shirt	ASTM D3776-85, ASTM D1777-64, ASTM D3786-87, ASTM D1682-64, ASTM D1117-80	TBD	TBD	TBD	TBD	●	●	●	TBD	◔	●	●	●
23	Tychem® QC Pants	ASTM D3776-85, ASTM D1777-64, ASTM D3786-87, ASTM D1682-64, ASTM D1117-80	TBD	TBD	TBD	TBD	●	●	●	NA	◔	●	●	●
37	Kappler CPF 4 Bib Overall	OSHA 1910.132 and OSHA 1910.120; ASTM D751 Test Battery	○	NA	◐	●	●	●	●	NA	TBD	●	●	TBD
39	Kappler CPF 4 Jacket	OSHA 1910.132 and OSHA 1910.120; ASTM D751 Test Battery	○	NA	◐	●	●	●	●	NA	TBD	●	●	TBD
41	Lakeland Tychem 10,000 Level B Overalls	Not specified	●	●	◐	●	●	●	●	NA	○	TBD	TBD	TBD
40	Lakeland Tychem 10,000 Level B Jacket	Not specified	●	●	◐	●	●	●	●	NA	○	TBD	TBD	TBD
44	Tyvek QC Level B Jacket	Not specified	TBD	TBD	TBD	TBD	●	●	◐	NA	○	●	●	TBD

'NA' - the specific selection factor is not applicable for the piece of equipment.
'TBD' (to be determined) - there is currently no data available to support that selection factor.
See Table 9-11 for selection factor definitions.
* See Appendix B, References, number eight.

Table 9-6. Percutaneous protection (shirts, pants, jackets, and overalls)
August 2001

ID #	Name	Certifications/Regulations*	Chemical Agents Protection	Biological Agents Protection	TIMs Protection	Duration of Protection	Environmental Conditions	Weight/Comfort	Dexterity/Mobility (Ease of Use)	Available Sizes	Visibility	Launderability	Training Requirements	Unit Cost
14	Tyvek® Shirt	ASTM D3776-85, ASTM D1777-64, ASTM D1682, ASTM D2261	NA	TBD	TBD	●	●	●	●	NA	○	●	●	●
17	Tyvek® Pants	ASTM D3776-85, ASTM D1682, ASTM D1682, ASTM D2261	NA	TBD	TBD	●	●	●	●	NA	○	●	●	●
22	Tychem® QC Shirt	ASTM D3776-85, ASTM D3786-87, ASTM D1682-64, ASTM D1117-80	TBD	TBD	TBD	●	●	●	●	TBD	◔	●	●	●
23	Tychem® QC Pants	ASTM D3776-85, ASTM D3786-87, ASTM D1682-64, ASTM D1117-80	TBD	TBD	TBD	●	●	●	●	NA	◔	●	●	●
37	Kappler CPF 4 Bib Overall	OSHA 1910.132 and OSHA 1910.120; ASTM D751 Test Battery	○	NA	●	●	●	●	●	NA	TBD	●	●	TBD
39	Kappler CPF 4 Jacket	OSHA 1910.132 and OSHA 1910.120; ASTM D751 Test Battery	○	NA	●	●	●	●	●	NA	TBD	●	●	TBD
41	Lakeland Tychem 10,000 Level B Overalls	Not specified	●	●	●	●	●	●	●	NA	○	TBD	TBD	TBD
40	Lakeland Tychem 10,000 Level B Jacket	Not specified	●	●	●	●	●	●	●	NA	○	TBD	TBD	TBD
44	Tyvek QC Level B Jacket	Not specified	TBD	TBD	TBD	●	●	●	◐	NA	○	●	●	TBD

'NA' - the specific selection factor is not applicable for the piece of equipment.
'TBD' (to be determined) - there is currently no data available to support that selection factor.
See Table 9-11 for selection factor definitions.
* See Appendix B, References, number eight.

93

Table 9-7. Percutaneous protection (aprons, labcoats, and ponchos)
August 2001

ID #	Name	Certifications/Regulations*	Chemical Agents Protection	Biological Agents Protection	TIMs Protection	Duration of Protection	Environmental Conditions	Weight/Comfort	Dexterity/Mobility (Ease of Use)	Available Sizes	Visibility	Launderability	Training Requirements	Unit Cost
12	Tyvek® Labcoat	ASTM D3776-85, ASTM D1777-64, ASTM D1682, ASTM D2261	NA	TBD	TBD	●	●	●	●	NA	○	●	●	
13	Tyvek® Labcoat	ASTM D3776-85, ASTM D1777-64, ASTM D1682, ASTM D2261	NA	TBD	TBD	●	●	●	●	NA	○	●	●	
15	Tyvek® Labcoat	ASTM D3776-85, ASTM D1777-64, ASTM D1682, ASTM D2261	NA	TBD	TBD	●	●	●	●	NA	○	●	●	
16	Tyvek® Labcoat	ASTM D3776-85, ASTM D1777-64, ASTM D1682, ASTM D2261	NA	TBD	TBD	●	●	●	●	NA	○	●	●	
21	Tychem® QC Labcoat	ASTM D3776-85, ASTM D1777-64, ASTM D3788-87, ASTM D1682-64, ASTM D1117-80	TBD	TBD	TBD	●	●	●	●	NA	◔	●	●	
31	NBC Cover Poncho	Ministry of Defense, Austria; Test data can be obtained on request	●	◐	●	●	●	●	◐	NA	●	●	●	
43	Lakeland Tychem 10,000 Level B Apron	TBD	●	◐	●	●	●	●	●	NA	○	TBD	TBD	
50	Tychem SL Level B Apron	TBD	◐	TBD	●	●	●	●	○	NA	○	●	●	
56	Lakeland Tychem 9400 Level B Apron	TBD	●	◐	●	●	●	●	◐	NA	○	●	●	
61	PONCHO NP/60	TBD	●	TBD	◐	TBD	●	●	TBD	NA	TBD	TBD	TBD	

'NA' - the specific selection factor is not applicable for the piece of equipment.
'TBD' (to be determined) - there is currently no data available to support that selection factor.
See Table 9-11 for selection factor definitions.
* See Appendix B, References, number eight.

94

Table 9-8. Percutaneous protection (undergarments)
August 2001

ID #	Name	Certifications/Regulations*	Chemical Agents Protection	Biological Agents Protection	TIMs Protection	Duration of Protection	Environmental Conditions	Weight/Comfort	Dexterity/Mobility (Ease of Use)	Available Sizes	Visibility	Launderability	Training Requirements	Unit Cost
59	Chemical Protective Undergarment (CPU)	Military Specification MIL-U-44435; AVLAG Test Operating Procedure (TOP) 8-2-501	●	TBD	●	●	●	●	●	NA	◐	●	TBD	
67	Saratoga Chemical Protective Undergarment	MIL-C-29462; Independent test data/certificate of compliance is available upon request	●	◐	TBD	●	●	●	◐	NA	◐	●	○	

'NA' - the specific selection factor is not applicable for the piece of equipment.
'TBD' (to be determined) - there is currently no data available to support that selection factor.
See Table 9-11 for selection factor definitions.
* See Appendix B, References, number eight.

Table 9-9. Percutaneous protection (casualty bags)
August 2001

ID #	Name	Certifications/Regulations*	Chemical Agents Protection	Biological Agents Protection	TIMs Protection	Duration of Protection	Environmental Conditions	Weight/Comfort	Dexterity/Mobility (Ease of Use)	Available Sizes	Visibility	Launderability	Training Requirements	Unit Cost
32	NBC-Casualty Bag	Ministry of Defense, Austria; Test data can be obtained on request.	●	●	◐	●	●	●	◐	NA	●	●	●	◐
36	Casualty Bag	Canadian Department of National Defence; Available from Irvin Aerospace Canada Ltd.	●	○	TBD	●	○	●	NA	NA	◔	●	●	○
69	Weapons of Mass Destruction (WMD) Contamination Containment Bag	NA	●	●	◐	●	●	●	◐	NA	◔	●	●	◐

'NA' - the specific selection factor is not applicable for the piece of equipment.
'TBD' (to be determined) - there is currently no data available to support that selection factor.
See Table 9-11 for selection factor definitions.
* See Appendix B, References, number eight.

Table 9-10. Percutaneous protection (personal cooling)
August 2001

# ID	Name	Certifications/Regulations*	Chemical Agents Protection	Biological Agents Protection	TIMs Protection	Duration of protection	Environmental Conditions	Weight/Comfort	Dexterity/Mobility (Ease of Use)	Available Sizes	Visibility	Launderability	Training Requirements	Unit Cost
71	ILC Model 15 Cool Vest	NA	NA	NA	NA	●	●	●	●	○	NA	●	●	◐
72	ILC Model 19 Cool Vest	Type Classified by United States Army, 1997	NA	NA	NA	●	●	◐	●	○	NA	●	●	◐
73	Personal Ice Cooling System (PICS)	NA	NA	NA	NA	●	●	◐	●	●	NA	●	◐	○
74	Flexi ICE Cold Vest	NA	NA	NA	NA	●	●	●	●	◐	NA	●	TBD	TBD

NA - the specific selection factor is not applicable for the piece of equipment.
'TBD' (to be determined) - there is currently no data available to support that selection factor.
See Table 9-11 for selection factor definitions.
* See Appendix B, References, number eight.

97

Table 9-11. Selection factor key for percutaneous protective equipment (apparel)
August 2001

Symbol	Chemical Agents Protection	Biological Agents Protection	TIMs Protection	Duration of Protection	Environmental Conditions	Weight/Comfort	Dexterity/Mobility (Ease of Use)	Sizes Available (Hoods and Aprons)	Sizes Available (Garments)	Visibility	Launderability	Training Requirements	Cost (Hoods)	Cost (Foot Protection)	Cost (Hand and Arm Protection)	Cost (Other)
● (full)	Protects against all nerve and blister agents	Protects against all biological agents	Protects against all TIMs listed	Protects up to 2 h	Protects in all environments	Easily manageable, able to be worn for long periods with no effects	Not limiting	One size fits all	Many available sizes	90 % to 100 % visibility	Able to be cleaned and reused greater than 50 times	Little to no training required	Less than or equal to $500 per unit	Less than or equal to $100 per unit	Less than or equal to $75 for single unit or $150 for bulk packaging	Less than or equal to $75 for single unit or $150 for bulk packaging
◕ (three-quarter)										75 % to 90 % visibility	Able to be cleaned and reused 25 to 50 times					
◑ (half)	Protects against some of the nerve and blister agents	Protects against some biological agents	Protects against multiple TIMs	Protects 30 min to 90 min	Protects in normal environments	Manageable, but unable to wear for more than 1 h to 2 h at a time	Some loss of mobility, range of motion		Small, medium, and large	50 % to 75 % visibility	Able to be cleaned and reused 5 to 50 times	Some training required, 4 h or more	Greater than $500 but less than $1000 per unit	Greater than $100 but less than $500 per unit	Greater than $75 (single unit) or $150 (bulk) but less than $300 for single item or bulk packaging	Greater than $75 (single unit) or $150 (bulk) but less than $300 for single item or bulk packaging
◔ (quarter)											Not intended for reuse, but can be hand cleaned to remove dirt and dust					
○ (empty)	Protects against none of the blister or nerve agents	Protects against no biological agents	Protects against none of the TIMs listed	Protects less than 30 min	Protects only specific environments	Very heavy and cumbersome, unable to wear for prolonged periods	Very limiting	One size fits all	Numerous sizes, requires fit test	Less than 50 % visibility	Unable to be reused	Continuous training required with recertification every few months	Greater than or equal to $1000 per unit	Greater than or equal to $500 per unit	Greater than or equal to $300 for single unit or bulk packaging	Greater than or equal to $300 for single unit or bulk packaging

The blank cells designate that the symbol is not applicable for the selection factor.

APPENDIX A—RECOMMENDED QUESTIONS ON PERSONAL PROTECTIVE EQUIPMENT

APPENDIX A—RECOMMENDED QUESTIONS ON PERSONAL PROTECTION EQUIPMENT[1]

Buying detection, protection, decontamination, and communication equipment to respond to the threatened terrorist use of chemical or biological warfare agents may be new for public safety agencies. To help procurement officials obtain the best value for their domestic preparedness dollar, the staff of the Center for Domestic Preparedness (Fort McClellan, AL), military Chemical/Biological Units, the National Institute of Justice, and members of a Federal Inter Agency Board (that includes representatives from the State and local law enforcement, medical, and fire communities) have compiled a series of questions. These questions should assist officials in selecting products from the large number in the present day marketplace. Requesting vendors to provide written responses to your specific questions may also be helpful in the decision process.

1. What chemical warfare agents, toxic industrial chemicals, and biological agents has the equipment been tested against?
2. What were the testing procedures and standards NFPA, ASTM, NIOSH, U.S. Military Standards, NATO, European Standards, MILSPEC?
3. Who conducted the tests and when? Have the test results been verified by an independent laboratory or only by the manufacturer?
4. What types of tests were conducted—spray, vapor, man-in-simulant (MIST)?
5. Were respirators, suits, gloves, and boots tested against the agents individually or as part of an integrated ensemble?
6. Is the test data available? Where? How can I get a copy? Curves showing concentration as a function of time are better than just a single breakthrough time.
7. Was the equipment ever used in live agent testing? Who did the testing and is the data available?
8. What is the fabric used to make the suits? How are the seams put together? Simple sewn seams are weakest, covered or bound seams are better.
9. What are the breaking strength and tear strengths of the fabrics? How was the equipment wear and tear tested?
10. If the manufacturer recommends sealing seams with tape, ask why and whether that was the configuration the suit was tested in?
11. How flammable is the fabric and how quickly will a hot ember melt through the fabric compromising protection? Is there an aluminized version or overcover for use where there is a fire threat in addition to the toxic agent?
12. How long does it take to don the equipment and can one person do it or is a buddy system required? Does the equipment allow sufficient operational flexibility to do the job to include use of firearms?
13. What boot and glove sizes are available? Does suit sizing consider people with special builds? For suits, ask for nominal heights and weights—one size does not fit all!
14. What training is required to fit face masks? Does the company provide those services and how frequently? How do the masks accommodate prescription glasses, long hair or facial hair?

---

[1]The information in Appendix A was provided by the National Domestic Preparedness Office (NDPO) in coordination with the National Institute of Justice and the Technical Support Working Group.

15. How long can responder safely work in the suit at 50 °F, at 70 °F and at 90 °F? Are cooling suits available to help manage heat stress? How much do they cost and what are the maintenance requirements? Do the cooling suits require any penetrations of the suit?

16. Can the protective equipment be decontaminated after use or must it be disposed of? What are the decon and sampling procedures? What tests are required to verify that protection capability has not been compromised in the process? What are the procedures and costs for disposing of used equipment, for example spent mask filters?

17. How long has the company/manufacturer been involved with the Chem-Bio-Nuc and first responder industries?

18. Ask for names and phone numbers of departments currently using the company's equipment. Ask to follow-up on the phone any written testimonials.

19. What additional items are required to operate/maintain the equipment? At what cost?

20. What training materials are provided—manuals, videotapes? Are less expensive training suits available? Is there a chart available identifying PPE requirements as a function of agents and concentrations?

21. What type of warranty/maintenance support is offered? Cost?

22. What is the return rate on the equipment under warranty? What are the top five reasons for failure?

23. What similar companies' products has this product been tested against?

24. What is the shelf life for the equipment? (Open-exposed, closed-exposed, open-unexposed, closed-unexposed). What is the recommended storage procedure after opening (hanging, folded, etc.)? What factors, if any, decrease shelf life (UV, critical temperature…)?

25. What are the environmental limitations—high temp, low temp, humidity, sand/dust, or broken glass?

APPENDIX B—REFERENCES

APPENDIX B—REFERENCES

1. Armando S. Bevelacqua and Richard H. Stilp, *Terrorism Handbook for Operational Responders*, Emergency Film Group, Edgartown, MA, January 1998.

2. Robert E. Hunt, Timothy Hayes, and Warren B. Carroll, *Guidelines for Mass Casualty Decontamination During a Terrorist Chemical Agent Incident*, Battelle, Columbus, OH, September 1999.

3. A.K. Stuempfle, D.J. Howells, S.J. Armour, and C.A. Boulet, *International Task Force 25: Hazard from Industrial Chemicals Final Report*, Edgewood Research Development and Engineering Center, Aberdeen Proving Ground, MD, AD-B236562, ERDEC-SP-061, April 1998.

4. *Responding to a Biological or Chemical Threat: A Practical Guide*, U.S. Department of State, Bureau of Diplomatic Security, Washington, DC, 1996.

5. *2000 Emergency Response Guidebook, A Guidebook for First Responders During the Initial Phase of a Dangerous Goods/Hazardous Materials Incident*, U.S. Department of Transportation, Research and Special Programs Administration, Tempest Publishing, Alexandria, VA, January 2000.

6. *Potential Military Chemical/Biological Agents and Compounds*, FM 3-9, AFR 355-7; NAVFAC P-467, Army Chemical School, Fort McClellan, AL, December 12, 1990.

7. B. Newman, *Opening the Case of the Poison Umbrella*. The Wall Street Journal, May 24, 1991.

8. Information on equipment regulatory and/or certifying authorities listed in tables in sections 7, 8, and 9 can be found at the following websites:

   http://www.cdc.gov/

   http://www.cdc.gov/niosh/homepage.html

   http://www.osha-slc.gov/html/subject-index.html

   http://www.osha-slc.gov/

   http://www.cdc.gov/other.htm

   http://www.nfpa.org/Home/index.asp

   http://www.osha-slc.gov/dts/osta/otm/otm_viii/otm_viii_1.html

APPENDIX C—IMMEDIATELY DANGEROUS TO LIFE AND HEALTH (IDLH) VALUES

Chemical Warfare Agent	IDLH (ppm)[*]
GA/Tabun	0.03
GB/Sarin	0.03
GD/Soman	0.008
VX	0.002
H/Mustard	0.0004
L/Lewisite	0.0003

TIMs	IDLH (ppm)
1,2-Dimethylhydrazine	15
Acetone cyanohydrin	**
Acrolein	2
Acrylonitrile	85
Allyl alcohol	20
Allyl chlorocarbonate	
Allyl isothiocyanate	
Allylamine	
Ammonia	300
Arsenic trichloride	
Arsine	3
Boron tribromide	
Boron trichloride	ND
Boron trifluoride	25
Bromine	3
Bromine chloride	
Bromine pentafluoride	
Bromine trifluoride	
Carbon disulfide	500
Carbon monoxide	1200
Carbonyl fluoride	
Carbonyl sulfide	
Chlorine	10
Chlorine pentafluoride	
Chlorine trifluoride	20
Chloroacetaldehyde	45
Chloroacetone	
Chloroacetonitrile	
Chloroacetyl chloride	
Chlorosulfonic acid	
Crotonaldehyde	50
Cyanogen chloride	
Diborane	15
Diketene	
Dimethyl sulfate	7
Diphenylmethane-4,4'-diisocyanate	

---

[*] parts per million (ppm).
** Blank fields not determined.

TIMs	IDLH (ppm)
Ethyl phosphonic dichloride	
Ethyl phosphonothioic dichloride	
Ethyl chloroformate	
Ethyl chlorothiolformate	
Ethylene dibromide	100
Ethylene oxide	800
Ethyleneimine	100
Fluorine	25
Formaldehyde	20
Hexachlorocyclopentadiene	
Hydrogen bromide	30
Hydrogen chloride	50
Hydrogen cyanide	50
Hydrogen fluoride	30
Hydrogen iodide	
Hydrogen selenide	1
Hydrogen sulfide	100
Iron pentacarbonyl	
Isobutyl chloroformate	
Isopropyl chloroformate	
Isopropyl isocyanate	
Methanesulfonyl chloride	
Methyl bromide	250
Methyl chloroformate	
Methyl chlorosilane	
Methyl hydrazine	20
Methyl isocyanate	3
Methyl mercaptan	150
n-Butyl chloroformate	
n-Butyl isocyanate	
Nitric acid, fuming	25
Nitric oxide	100
Nitrogen dioxide	20
n-Propyl chloroformate	
Parathion	0.8
Perchloromethyl mercaptan	10
Phosgene	2
Phosphine	50
Phosphorus oxychloride	
Phosphorus pentafluoride	
Phosphorus trichloride	25
sec-Butyl chloroformate	
Selenium hexafluoride	2
Silicon tetrafluoride	
Stibine	5
Sulfur dioxide	100
Sulfur trioxide	1

TIMs	IDLH (ppm)
Sulfuric acid	4
Sulfuryl chloride	
Sulfuryl fluoride	200
Tellurium hexafluoride	1
tert-Butyl isocyanate	
n-Octyl mercaptan	
Tetraethyl lead	3
Tetraethyl pyrophosphate	0.4
Tetramethyl lead	3
Titanium tetrachloride	
Toluene 2,4-diisocyanate	2.5
Toluene 2,6-diisocyanate	2.5
Trichloroacetyl chloride	
Trifluoroacetyl chloride	
Tungsten hexafluoride	

ABOUT THE LAW ENFORCEMENT AND CORRECTIONS STANDARDS AND TESTING PROGRAM

The Law Enforcement and Corrections Standards and Testing Program is sponsored by the Office of Science and Technology of the National Institute of Justice (NIJ), U.S. Department of Justice. The program responds to the mandate of the Justice System Improvement Act of 1979, directed NIJ to encourage research and development to improve the criminal justice system and to disseminate the results to Federal, State, and local agencies.

The Law Enforcement and Corrections Standards and Testing Program is an applied research effort that determines the technological needs of justice system agencies, sets minimum performance standards for specific devices, tests commercially available equipment against those standards, and disseminates the standards and the test results to criminal justice agencies nationally and internationally.

The program operates through:

The *Law Enforcement and Corrections Technology Advisory Council* (LECTAC), consisting of nationally recognized criminal justice practitioners from Federal, State, and local agencies, which assesses technological needs and sets priorities for research programs and items to be evaluated and tested.

The *Office of Law Enforcement Standards* (OLES) at the National Institute of Standards and Technology, which develops voluntary national performance standards for compliance testing to ensure that individual items of equipment are suitable for use by criminal justice agencies. The standards are based upon laboratory testing and evaluation of representative samples of each item of equipment to determine the key attributes, develop test methods, and establish minimum performance requirements for each essential attribute. In addition to the highly technical standards, OLES also produces technical reports and user guidelines that explain in nontechnical terms the capabilities of available equipment.

The *National Law Enforcement and Corrections Technology Center* (NLECTC), operated by a grantee, which supervises a national compliance testing program conducted by independent laboratories. The standards developed by OLES serve as performance benchmarks against which commercial equipment is measured. The facilities, personnel, and testing capabilities of the independent laboratories are evaluated by OLES prior to testing each item of equipment, and OLES helps the NLECTC staff review and analyze data. Test results are published in Equipment Performance Reports designed to help justice system procurement officials make informed purchasing decisions.

Publications are available at no charge through the National Law Enforcement and Corrections Technology Center. Some documents are also available online through the Internet/World Wide Web. To request a document or additional information, call 800–248–2742 or 301–519–5060, or write:

National Law Enforcement and Corrections Technology Center
P.O. Box 1160
Rockville, MD 20849–1160
E-Mail: *asknlectc@nlectc.org*
World Wide Web address: *http://www.nlectc.org*

This document is not intended to create, does not create, and may not be relied upon to create any rights, substantive or procedural, enforceable at law by any party in any matter civil or criminal.

Opinions or points of view expressed in this document represent a consensus of the authors and do not represent the official position or policies of the U.S. Department of Justice. The products and manufacturers discussed in this document are presented for informational purposes only and do not constitute product approval or endorsement by the U.S. Department of Justice.

The National Institute of Justice is a component of the Office of Justice Programs, which also includes the Bureau of Justice Assistance, the Bureau of Justice Statistics, the Office of Juvenile Justice and Delinquency Prevention, and the Office for Victims of Crime.